China's Currency Policy: An Analysis of the Economic Issues

Wayne M. Morrison
Specialist in Asian Trade and Finance

Marc Labonte
Specialist in Macroeconomic Policy

December 19, 2011

Congressional Research Service

7-5700

www.crs.gov

RS21625

CRS Report for Congress ─────────────────────────

Prepared for Members and Committees of Congress

Summary

China's policy of intervening in currency markets to limit or halt the appreciation of its currency, the renminbi (RMB), against the U.S. dollar and other currencies has become an issue of concern for many in Congress. Critics charge that China's currency policy is intended to make its exports significantly less expensive, and its imports more expensive, than would occur if the RMB were a freely-traded currency. They contend that the RMB is significantly undervalued against the dollar and that this has been a major contributor to the large annual U.S. trade deficits with China and the loss of U.S. jobs in recent years. Several bills have been introduced the 112th Congress that seek to address the effects of undervalued currencies (which are largely aimed at China), including H.R. 639, S. 328, S. 1130, S. 1267, and S. 1619 (which passed the Senate on October 11, 2011). On the other hand, some analysts contend that China's industrial policies, its failure to adequately protect U.S. intellectual property rights, and its unbalanced economic growth model, pose more serious challenges to U.S. economic interests than China's currency policy. Some U.S. business groups have also expressed concern that U.S. currency legislation could aggravate U.S.-China commercial ties.

From July 2005 to July 2008, China's central bank allowed the RMB to appreciate against the dollar by about 21%. However, once the effects of the global economic crisis became apparent in 2008, China halted appreciation of the RMB in an effort to help Chinese industries dependent on trade. From July 2008 to about mid-June 2010, China kept the exchange rate of the RMB relatively constant at 6.83 yuan (the base unit of the RMB) to the dollar. On June 19, 2010, China resumed appreciation of the RMB, and since then, China has allowed the RMB/dollar exchange rate to rise by 7.6% (to 6.35 yuan per dollar) through November 30, 2011. However, many U.S. officials have criticized this pace as being too slow, especially given China's strong economic growth over the past few years, including its trade sector, and its rising level of foreign exchange reserves.

Many economists argue that the effects of China's currency policy on the U.S. economy are complex. If the RMB is undervalued (as many contend), then it might be viewed as an indirect export subsidy which artificially lowers the prices of Chinese products imported into the United States. Under this view, this benefits U.S. consumers and U.S. firms that use Chinese-made parts and components, but could negatively affect certain U.S. import-sensitive firms. An undervalued RMB might also have the effect of limiting the level of U.S. exports to China than might occur under a floating exchange rate system. Further complicating the issue is China's large purchases of U.S. Treasury securities, which totaled at least $1.15 trillion as of September 2011. These purchases occur because China's intervention in currency markets causes it to accumulate large levels of foreign exchange reserves, especially U.S. dollars, which are then used to purchase U.S. debt. Such purchases help the U.S. government fund its budget deficit, which helps to keep U.S. interest rates relatively low. These factors suggest that an appreciation of the RMB to the dollar could benefit some U.S. sectors, but could negatively affect others. The effects of the global economic slowdown have refocused attention on the need to reduce global imbalances (in savings, investment, and trade), especially between China and the United States. Many economists contend that China should take steps to rebalance its economy by lessening its dependence on exports and fixed investment as the main drivers of its economic growth while boosting the level of domestic consumer demand. A market-based currency policy is seen as an important factor in achieving this goal. Further RMB appreciation could help promote the development of non-export industries in China, while boosting China's imports, including from the United States.

Contents

Figures

Tables

Appendixes

Contacts

Introduction and Overview of the Currency Issue

China's policy of intervention to limit the appreciation of its currency, the renminbi (RMB), or yuan, against the dollar and other currencies has become a major source of tension with many of its trading partners, especially the United States.[1] Some analysts contend that China deliberately "manipulates" its currency in order to gain unfair trade advantages over its trading partners. They further argue that China's undervalued currency has been a major factor in the large annual U.S. trade deficits with China and has contributed to widespread job losses in the United States, especially in manufacturing. President Obama stated in February 2010 that China's undervalued currency puts U.S. firms at a "huge competitive disadvantage," and he pledged to make addressing China's currency policy a top priority.[2] At a news conference in November 2011, President Obama stated that China needed to "go ahead and move towards a market-based system for their currency" and that the United States and other countries felt that "enough is enough."[3] Several bills to address China's currency have been introduced in the 112th Congress, including S. 1619, which passed the Senate on October 11, 2011. The bill would apply a number of measures against certain countries that are deemed to have a currency that is deemed to be in "fundamental misalignment."

The RMB has appreciated by 30.4% against the dollar between July 2005 (when significant Chinese exchange rate reforms were begun) and November 30, 2011, although this has occurred at a gradual pace, and, over some periods, the RMB was held constant against the dollar. The pace of RMB appreciation has been criticized by many of China's trading partners, including the United States, as being too slow, and many contend that the RMB remains significantly undervalued. Although economists differ as to the economic effects an undervalued RMB has on the United States (many cite both positive and negative effects), most agree that currency flexibility would be an important factor in helping to reduce global imbalances, which are believed to have been a major factor that sparked the global financial crisis and economic slowdown. They further contend that currency reform is in China's own long-term economic interest. China has pledged to continue to make its currency policy more flexible, but has expressed concerns that appreciating the RMB too quickly could cause significant job losses (especially in China's export sectors), which could disrupt the economy.

Some economists question whether RMB appreciation would produce significant net benefits for the U.S. economy. They argue that prices for Chinese products would rise, which would hurt U.S. consumers and U.S. firms that use imported Chinese components in their production. In addition, an appreciating RMB might lessen the Chinese government's need to purchase U.S. Treasury securities, which could affect U.S. real interest rates. It is further argued that an appreciating currency would do little to shift manufacturing done by foreign-invested firms (including U.S. firms) in China to the United States; instead, such firms would likely shift production to other low-cost East Asian countries. Finally, it is argued that an appreciating RMB might boost some U.S. exports to China, but the effects of lower prices for U.S. products in China could be negated to a large extent by China's restrictive trade and investment barriers. Such analysts view currency

---

[1] The official name of China's currency is the renminbi (RMB), which is denominated in yuan units. Both RMB and yuan are used interchangeably to describe China's currency.

[2] The White House, *Remarks by the President at the Senate Democratic Policy Committee Issues Conference*, February 3, 2010.

[3] The White House, *News Conference by President Obama*, November 14, 2011.

---

reform as part of a broad set of goals that U.S. trade policy should pursue. These goals include inducing China to: rebalance its economy by making consumer demand, rather than fixed investment and exporting, the main sources of China's economic growth; eliminate industrial policies that seek to promote and protect Chinese firms (especially state-owned firms); reduce trade and investment barriers; and improve protection of U.S. intellectual property rights.

This report provides an overview of the economic issues surrounding the current debate over China's currency policy. It identifies the economic costs and benefits of China's currency policy for both China and the United States, and possible implications if China were to allow its currency to significantly appreciate or to float freely. It also examines proposed legislation in the 112th Congress that seeks to address China's currency policy.

Background on China's Currency Policy

Prior to 1994, China maintained a dual exchange rate system. This consisted of an official fixed exchange rate system (which was used by the government), and a relatively market-based exchange rate system that was used by importers and exporters in "swap markets," although access to foreign exchange was highly restricted in order to limit imports, resulting in a large black market for foreign exchange. The two exchange rates differed significantly. The official exchange rate with the dollar in 1993 was 5.77 yuan versus 8.70 yuan in the swap markets. China's dual exchange rate system was criticized by the United States because of the restrictions it (and other policies) placed on foreign imports.

In 1994, the Chinese government unified the two exchange rate systems at an initial rate of 8.70 yuan to the dollar, which eventually was allowed to rise to 8.28 by 1997 and was then kept relatively constant until July 2005. The RMB became largely convertible on a current account (trade) basis, but not on a capital account basis, meaning that yuan are not regularly obtainable for investment purposes. From 1994 until July 2005, China maintained a policy of pegging the RMB to the U.S. dollar at an exchange rate of roughly 8.28 yuan to the dollar. The peg appears to have been largely intended to promote a relatively stable environment for foreign trade and investment in China (since such a policy prevents large swings in exchange rates)—a policy utilized by many developing countries in their early development stages. The Chinese central bank maintained this peg by buying (or selling) as many dollar-denominated assets in exchange for newly printed yuan as needed to eliminate excess demand (supply) for the yuan. As a result, the exchange rate between the RMB and the dollar basically stayed the same, despite changing economic factors which could have otherwise caused the yuan to appreciate (or depreciate) relative to the dollar. Under a floating exchange rate system, the relative demand for the two countries' goods and assets would determine the exchange rate of the RMB to the dollar.

2005: China Reforms the Peg

The Chinese government modified its currency policy on July 21, 2005. It announced that the RMB's exchange rate would become "adjustable, based on market supply and demand with reference to exchange rate movements of currencies in a basket,"[4] and that the exchange rate of

---

[4] It was later announced that the composition of the basket would include the dollar, the yen, the euro, and a few other currencies, although the currency composition of the basket has never been revealed. If the value of the yuan were determined according to a basket of currencies, however, it would not have shown the stability it has had against the
(continued...)

the U.S. dollar against the RMB would be adjusted from 8.28 yuan to 8.11, an appreciation of 2.1%. Unlike a true floating exchange rate, the RMB would be allowed to fluctuate by up to 0.3% (later changed to 0.5%) on a daily basis against the basket.

After July 2005, China allowed the RMB to appreciate steadily, but very slowly. From July 21, 2005 to July 21, 2008, the dollar-RMB exchange rate went from 8.11 to 6.83, an appreciation of 18.7% (or 20.8% if the initial 2.1% appreciation of the RMB to the dollar is included). The situation at this time might be best described as a "managed float"—market forces determined the general direction of the RMB's movement, but the government retarded its rate of appreciation through market intervention.

Figure 1. Nominal RMB/Dollar Exchange Rate: January 2008 to May 2010

(yuan per U.S. dollar [monthly averages])

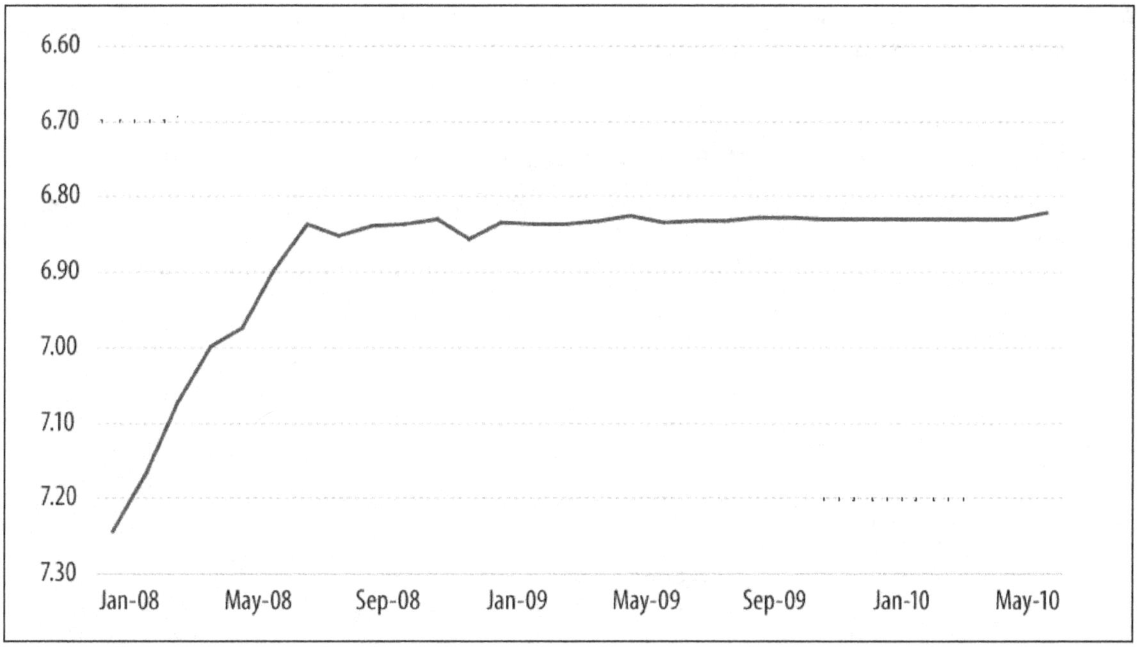

Source: Global Insight.

Note: Chart inverted for illustrative purposes. A rising line indicates appreciation of the RMB to the dollar and a falling line indicates depreciation.

2008: RMB Appreciation is Suspended

China halted its currency appreciation policy around mid-July 2008 (see **Figure 1**), mainly because of declining global demand for Chinese products that resulted from the effects of the global financial crisis. In 2009, Chinese exports and imports fell by 15.9% and 11.3% over 2008 levels. The Chinese government reported that thousands of export-oriented factories were shut down and that over 20 million migrant workers lost their jobs in 2009 because of the direct

---

(...continued)

dollar between mid-2008 and mid-2010, unless the basket were overwhelmingly weighted toward dollars.

effects of the global economic slowdown. The RMB/dollar exchange rate was held relatively constant at 6.83 through around mid-June 2010.

2010: RMB Appreciation is Resumed

On June 19, 2010, China's central bank, the People's Bank of China (PBC), stated that, based on current economic conditions, it had decided to "proceed further with reform of the RMB exchange rate regime and to enhance the RMB exchange rate flexibility." It ruled out any large one-time revaluations, stating "it is important to avoid any sharp and massive fluctuations of the RMB exchange rate," in part so that Chinese corporations could more easily adjust (such as through upgrading) to an appreciation of the currency. Many observers contend the timing of the RMB announcement was intended in part to prevent China's currency policy from being a central focus of the G-20 summit in Toronto in June 2010. As indicated in **Figure 2**, the RMB's exchange rate with the dollar has gone up and down since RMB appreciation was resumed, but overall, it has appreciated.[5] From June 19, 2010 (when currency appreciation was resumed) to November 30, 2011, the yuan/dollar exchange rate rose from 6.83 to 6.35, an appreciation of 7.6%.

Figure 2. Average Monthly RMB-Dollar Exchange Rate: June 2010-November 2011

(yuan per U.S. dollar)

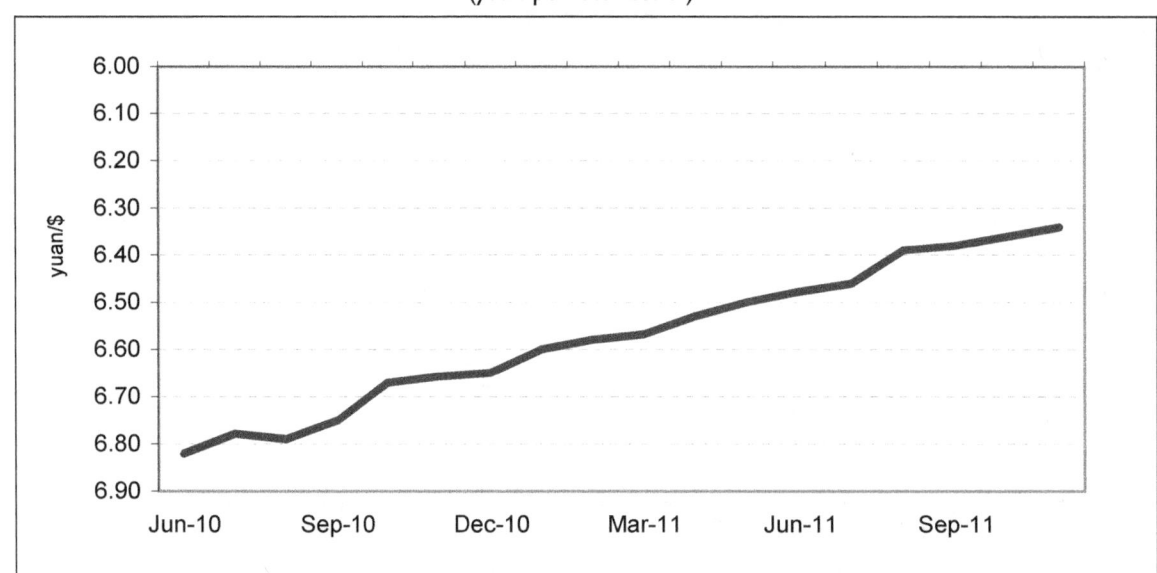

Source: China Money and Global Insight.

Notes: Chart inverted for illustrative purposes to show the appreciation or depreciation of the RMB against the dollar. Data are the Chinese government's official middle rate.

---

[5] The fact that the currency has appreciated some days but has depreciated on others raises a number of questions as to the extent and pace the PBC will allow the RMB to appreciate over time. Many observers believe that this is a sign that appreciation of the RMB will happen over a long period of time, but in an unpredictable way in an effort to limit RMB speculation and inflows of "hot money," which could destabilize China's economy.

Factoring in Inflation and Trade-Weighted Flows

Some economists contend that a more accurate measurement of the yuan/dollar exchange rate involves factoring in differences in inflation between China and the United States—the real exchange rate.[6] This approach is relevant because if prices are rising faster in China than in the United States, then the prices of Chinese tradable goods may be rising as well (even with no change in the nominal exchange rate). In effect, a higher Chinese inflation rate relative to the Unites States acts as a de facto appreciation of the RMB. From June 2010 to October 2011, Chinese average real monthly inflation was more than double the real average U.S. level.[7] Factoring in inflation into the RMB/dollar exchange rate indicates that the RMB appreciated in real terms by 10.2% from June 2010 to October 2011 (as opposed to a 7.4% increase measured on a nominal basis).

Other economists contend that evaluating whether a currency is undervalued should be based on an inflation-adjusted trade-weighted index, often referred to as the "effective exchange rate."[8] Such an index reflects overall changes in a country's exchange rate with its major trading partners—not just the United States. China's relative peg to the dollar has meant that as the dollar has depreciated or appreciated against a number of major currencies, the RMB has depreciated or appreciated against them as well. For example, from July 2008 to May 2010, when the RMB exchange rate to the dollar was kept constant (at 6.83 yuan per dollar), the real trade-weighted exchange rate of China's currency (based on its trade with 57 major economies) appreciated by 8.9%. However, between June 2010 (when appreciation of the RMB to the dollar was resumed) and July 2011, China's real trade-weighted exchange rate depreciated by 1.5% (see **Figure 3**), even though the RMB had appreciated against the dollar in real terms by 7.0%.[9] Thus, although the RMB appreciated against the U.S. dollar the overall effects of that appreciation for China were offset by the RMB's depreciation against the currencies of some of its other major trading partners in real terms. However, China's real trade-weighted exchange rate has risen sharply since July 2011.[10]

---

[6] The Department of the Treasury often includes estimates of the RMB's real (inflation-adjusted) exchange rate with the dollar in its biannual report on international economic and exchange rate policies.

[7] The Chinese and U.S. average real inflation rates during this period were 4.77% and 2.29%, respectively.

[8] A trade-weighted index is based on the relative amount (or percent) of a country's trade is with each of its major trading partners.

[9] During the same period, the trade-weighted exchange rate of the U.S. dollar against 57 economies depreciated by 9.7%.

[10] From January to October 2011, the trade-weighted exchange rate of the RMB increased by 7.0%.

Figure 3. Change in China's Real Trade-weighted Exchange Rate: July 2008-October 2011

(Index based on average annual 2005 data [2005 = 100])

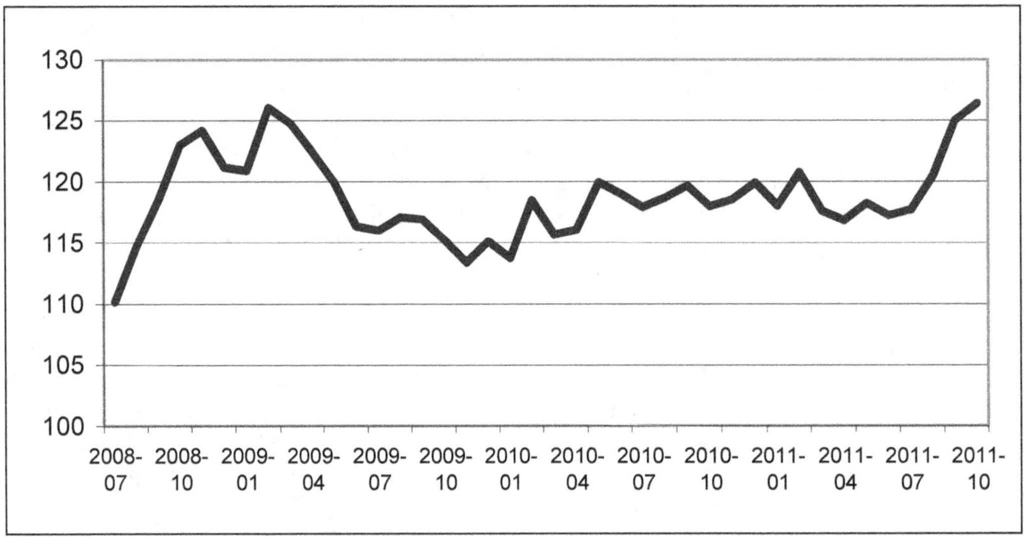

Source: Bank of International Settlements.

Note: Weights calculated based on China's trade with 57 economies. Inflation calculated using measurements of national consumer price indexes.

Concerns in the United States over China's Currency Policy: Trade Deficits and Jobs

Many U.S. policymakers and certain business and labor representatives have charged that the Chinese government "manipulates" its currency in order to make it significantly undervalued vis-à-vis the U.S. dollar, thus making Chinese exports to the United States less expensive, and U.S. exports to China more expensive, than they would be if exchange rates were determined by market forces.[11] They further contend that, while a pegged currency may have been appropriate during China's early stages of economic development, it can no longer be justified, given the size of China's economy and trade flows, and the impact these have on the global economy.[12]

Critics further argue that the undervalued currency has been a major factor behind the burgeoning U.S. trade deficit with China, which surged from $10 billion in 1990 to $273 billion in 2010, and is projected to reach about $295 billion in 2011. Other factors viewed by some as evidence of Chinese currency manipulation (and misalignment) are China's massive accumulation of foreign exchange reserves, which, on a year-end basis grew from $403 billion in 2003 to $2.85 trillion 2010,[13] and its large annual current account surpluses, which grew from $46 billion in 2003 to $412 billion in 2008, (see **Figure 4**).[14] In a July 2010 report, the International Monetary Fund

---

[11] In general, U.S.-invested firms in China do not appear to be as concerned over the value of China's currency relative to the dollar as are U.S. import-sensitive firms that compete with low-priced Chinese products.

[12] China emerged as the world's largest merchandise exporter in 2010, accounting for 10.1% of global exports. China also became the world's largest economy in 2010 on a nominal dollar basis.

[13] Those reserves reached $3.2 trillion at the end of September 2011.

[14] China's current account surplus peaked in 2008, declined to $261 billion in 2009 (due largely to the effects of the (continued...)

(IMF) warned that, over the medium-term, there was potential for sizable current account surpluses to return as China's policy stimulus is wound down and the global economy recovers.[15] The IMF's September 2011 *World Economic Outlook* projects that China's current account will rise from $305 billion in 2010 to $361 billion in 2011, and to $852 billion by 2016.[16] *Global Insight* predicts that China's foreign exchange reserves will increase to $4.6 trillion by the year 2014, which would be an increase of nearly $1.7 trillion over 2010 levels.[17]

Figure 4. China's Current Account Balance and Annual Change in Foreign Exchange Reserves: 2001-2010

($ billions)

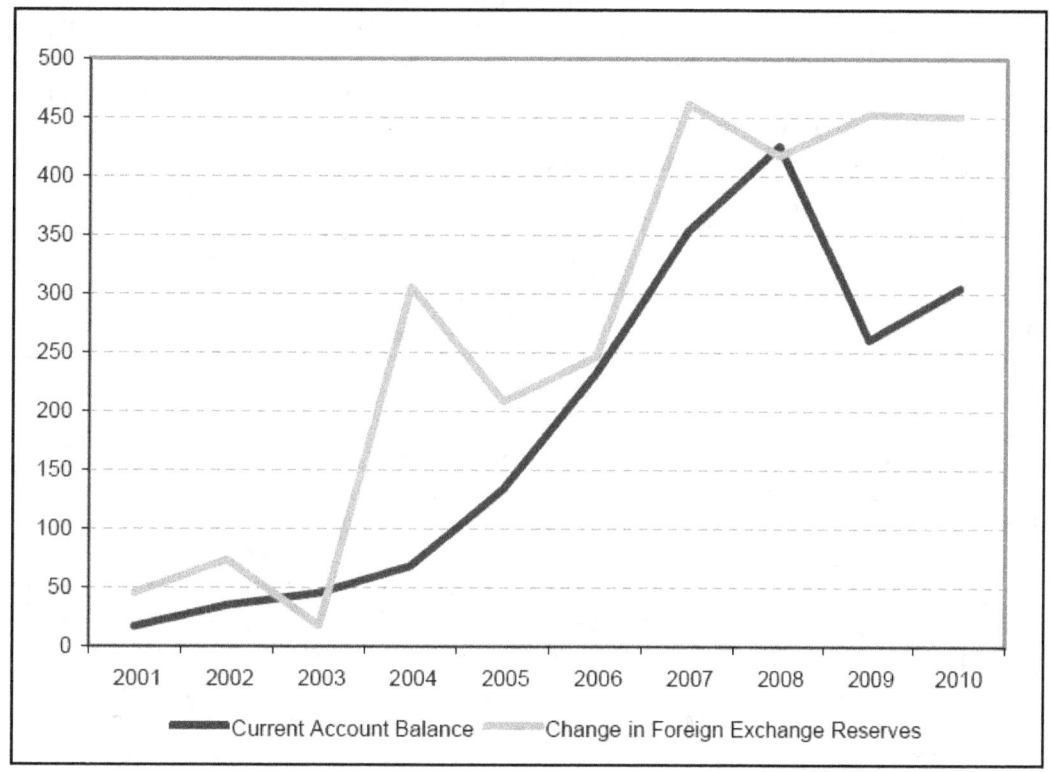

Source: Economist Intelligence Unit, IMF, and Chinese State Administration of Foreign Exchange.

The current high rate of unemployment in the United States appears to have intensified concerns over the perceived impact of China's currency policy on the U.S. economy, especially employment. Many have argued that RMB appreciation would boost the level of U.S. jobs.

(...continued)

global financial slowdown), and increased to $305 billion in 2010.

[15] IMF, *People's Republic of China: 2010 Article IV Consultation—Staff Report; Staff Statement; Public Information Notice on the Executive Board Discussion*, July 2010, p. 1.

[16] China's current account surplus as a percent of GDP is predicted by the IMF to rise from 5.2% in 2010 to 7.2% in 2016. See IMF, *World Economic Outlook Database, September 2011*.

[17] IHS Global Insight, *China, Interim Forecast*, updated August 2011.

Some analysts contend that there is a direct correlation between the U.S. trade deficit and U.S. job losses. For example, a study by the Economic Policy Institute (EPI) claims that the U.S. trade deficit with China (which EPI claims is largely the result of China's currency policy) led to the loss or displacement of 2.8 million jobs (of which, 69% were in manufacturing) between 2001 and 2010.[18] The EPI report states that, while U.S. exports to China support U.S. jobs, U.S. imports from China "displace American workers who would have been employed making these products in the United States."[19] The results of the EPI study were referenced by several Members during the Senate consideration of S. 1619 (discussed in the next section).

Some analysts contend that China's currency policy induces other East Asian economies to intervene in currency markets and keep their currencies weak against the dollar so they can compete with Chinese goods; this is viewed as preventing further depreciation of the dollar relative to other Asian currencies, and thus diminishing U.S. exports throughout Asia. Based on the assumption that China's currency is undervalued by at least 40% against the dollar and 25% on a trade-weighted basis, C. Fred Bergsten from the Peterson Institute for International Economics estimates that a market-based Chinese currency would result in a large appreciation of the RMB and other Asian currencies against the dollar (or in other words a depreciation of the dollar to Asian currencies), which would boost U.S. exports and generate an additional 600,000 to 1.2 million jobs in the United States.[20] U.S. economist Paul Krugman contends that the undervalued RMB has become a significant drag on global economic recovery, estimating that it has lowered global GDP by 1.4%, and has especially hurt poor countries.[21] Claims about the negative effect of China's exchange rate on U.S. employment and trade are often juxtaposed with the observation that China's economy has grown rapidly over the past thee years (real GDP grew at an average annual rate of nearly 10% from 2008 to 2010), while other countries experienced negative or stagnant growth. This has led some commentators to argue that China's exchange rate peg represents a "beggar thy neighbor" policy (i.e., meant to promote Chinese economic development at the expense of other countries) at a time of global economic crisis. (The validity of claims about the RMB's effect on the U.S. economy will be analyzed in the section below entitled "An Economic Analysis of the Effects of China's Currency .") Some analysts contend that a significant appreciation of the RMB would reduce the bilateral trade imbalance between China and the U.S.. For example, a report by Bloomberg Government estimated that a 7% annual real appreciation of the RMB to the dollar would cut the U.S. trade deficit with China in half by 2014.[22] The study assumes that RMB appreciation would result in the appreciation of other currencies as well, which would result in a sharp drop in the overall U.S. trade deficit from an estimated $368 billion in 2011 to $59 billion in 2014. Because of these factors, some Members contend that China should be cited by the Department of the Treasury as a country that manipulates its currency in order to gain an unfair trade advantage (see text box).

---

[18] Economic Policy Institute, *Growing U.S. trade deficit with China cost 2.8 million jobs between 2001 and 2010*, September 21, 2011, available at http://www.epi.org/publication/growing-trade-deficit-china-cost-2-8-million. Note, some have criticized the methodology used in the report, which assumes that the U.S. trade deficit with China has a direct and significant effect on the level of employment in the United States.

[19] Ibid., p. 8.

[20] C. Fred Bergsten, Peterson Institute for International Economics, Testimony before the Committee on Ways and Means, U.S. House of Representatives, March 24, 2010. In testimony to the House Committee on Ways and Means on September 15, 2010, Bergsten stated that "elimination of the Chinese misalignment would create about half a million US jobs." See testimony at http://www.iie.com/publications/testimony/bergsten20100915.pdf.

[21] New York Times, March 14, 2010, and December 31, 2009. Krugman also estimates that China's currency policy has caused 1.4 million job losses in the United States.

[22] Bloomberg Government, *A Higher Yuan Would Half the U.S.-China Trade Deficit*, December 2011.

Is China a "Currency Manipulator?"

The U.S. Department of the Treasury is required on a biannual basis to issue a *Report to Congress on International Economic and Exchange Rate Policies* of major U.S. trading partners,[23] and to "consider whether countries manipulate the rate of exchange between their currency and the United States dollar for purposes of preventing effective balance of payments adjustments or gaining unfair competitive advantage in international trade."[24] If such manipulation is found to exist with respect to countries that have material global current account surpluses and have significant bilateral trade surpluses with the United States, the Secretary of the Treasury is directed to initiate negotiations with such countries on an expedited basis in the International Monetary Fund or bilaterally, for the purpose of ensuring that such countries regularly and promptly adjust the rate of exchange between their currencies and the U.S. dollar to permit effective balance of payments adjustments and to eliminate the unfair advantage. China was cited as a currency manipulator five times by Treasury from May 1992 and July 1994 over such issues as its dual exchange rate system, periods of currency devaluation, restrictions on imports, and lack of access to foreign exchange by importers.

Many members of Congress have expressed frustration that Treasury has not cited China as a currency manipulator in recent years.[25] Observers note that the language in the statute is somewhat unclear as to what policies constitute actual currency manipulation (and the extent of Treasury's discretion to make such a determination). A 2005 Treasury Department report stated that such a determination under the guiding statute was "inherently difficult" because of the interplay of macroeconomic and microeconomic forces throughout the world, but said that such a designation could be made if the authorities of an economy "intentionally act to set the exchange rate at levels, or ranges, such that for a protracted period the exchange rate differs significantly from the rate that would have prevailed in the absence of action by the authorities."[26] A 2005 Government Accountability Office (GAO) report on the Treasury Department's currency reports stated that in order for Treasury to reach a positive determination of currency manipulation, a country would have to have a material global current account surplus and a significant bilateral trade surplus with the United States, and would have to be manipulating its currency with the "intent" of gaining a trade advantage. Some observers contend that Treasury will not cite China as a currency manipulator because it cannot prove that China's currency policy is "intended" to give it an unfair trade advantage, since Chinese government intervention in currency markets attempts to slow or halt the appreciation of the RMB (as opposed to sharply depreciating the RMB). Other observers contend that as long as China continues to take steps to make its currency more flexible, Treasury will refrain from citing China. A third theory states that citing China as a currency manipulator would have no practical effect (especially since China and the United States are already engaged on this issue at the highest government level) other than to "name and shame," a policy that could anger the Chinese government without producing any concrete results. However, some U.S. policy analysts and members of Congress have strongly urged the Treasury Department to designate China as a currency manipulator in order to "name and shame it." By doing so, it is argued, the United States would be sending a message that it was no longer willing to tolerate China's currency policy and it could encourage other countries to rally behind the U.S. position (including within the International Monetary Fund which exercises surveillance of its members currency policy), and could possibly lead to multilateral meeting/agreement on global exchange rate realignment.[27] Several bills have been introduced in Congress over the past few years that would attempt to limit the Treasury Department's discretion in taking action on undervalued currencies by requiring it to indentify certain misaligned currencies based on a specific criteria, regardless of intent of the currency policy.

---

[23] As required under §3004 of Omnibus Trade and Competitiveness Act of 1988 (22 U.S.C 5305).

[24] This language appears to have been taken from Article IV, §1 (iii) of the Articles of Agreement of the International Monetary Fund (IMF), which states that members should, among other things "avoid manipulating exchange rates or the international monetary system in order to prevent effective balance of payments adjustment or to gain an unfair competitive advantage over other members."

[25] Many members sharply criticized the Department of the Treasury's decision in April 2010 to delay issuing its first 2010 exchange rate report (usually issued in March or April). That report was issued on July 8, 2010 (after China made its announcement on currency reform) and it did not cite China (or any other country) for currency manipulation.

[26] U.S. Department of Treasury, *Semiannual Report on International Economic and Exchange Rate Policies, Appendix: Analysis of Exchange Rates Pursuant to the Act*, November 2005.

[27] Testimony by C. Fred Bergsten, Peterson Institute of International Economics, *Correcting the Chinese Exchange Rate: an Action Plan*, before the House Ways & Means Committee, March 24, 2010.

Legislative Proposals to Address Undervalued Currencies

Numerous bills have been introduced in Congress over the past several years that have sought to induce China (and other countries) to reform its currency policy or to address the perceived effects by that policy on the U.S. economy. For example, one bill introduced in the 108th Congress by Senator Schumer (S. 1586) sought to impose additional duties of 27.5% on imported Chinese products unless China appreciated its currency to market levels.

Over the past few years, some legislative proposals have sought to apply U.S. anti-dumping and countervailing duty measures to address the effects of China's undervalued currency, namely to treat it as an export subsidy (countervailing measures) or as a factor that is included in the determination of anti-dumping duties. This would likely increase U.S. countervailing and anti-dumping duties on certain imports from China. A major source of contention is whether such measures would be consistent with U.S. obligations in WTO. Some contend that the WTO allows countries (under certain conditions) to administer their own trade remedy laws, and thus they argue that making currency undervaluation a factor in determining countervailing or anti-dumping duties would be consistent with WTO rules. Critics of such proposals counter that WTO rules do not specifically include currency undervaluation as a factor that can be used to implement trade remedy actions, and thus, such proposals, if enacted, might be challenged by China (and possibly other WTO members) as a violation of WTO rules.[28]

Another major objective of various recent currency bills is to eliminate current provisions of U.S. trade laws that require the Treasury Department to identify countries that intentionally "manipulate" their currency. Treasury has not identified any country for manipulating its currency since 1994. Some bills have sought to create a process whereby Treasury would identify countries with currencies that were estimated to be fundamentally misaligned (based on certain criteria), regardless of intent. Such bills list a number of actions (some of which would be punitive) the U.S. government would be directed to take against certain "priority" countries.

Some supporters of currency legislation aimed at China hope that the introduction of such bills will induce China to appreciate its currency more rapidly. Opponents of the bill contend that such legislation could antagonize China and induce it to slow the rate of RMB appreciation. Another concern is that China might also retaliate against U.S. exports to China and/or U.S.-invested firms in China if such legislation became law.

Legislation in the 112th Congress

To date, five currency bills have been introduced in the 112th Congress, including H.R. 639, S. 328, S. 1130, S. 1238, S. 1619 (which was passed by the Senate in October 2011).

---

[28] Of particular concern to some groups are proposals that would require the U.S. government to calculate the percentage level of a currency's misalignment or undervaluation, since there is no universally-accepted method of making such estimates (see discussion of this issue on page 15). A September 22, 2011, letter sent by a group of U.S. business organizations to Senators Reid and McConnell argued that any legislation that requires the Commerce Department to estimate the "true" exchange rate would "create a process that will be highly subjective and potentially politicized." A copy of the letter can be found at http://businessroundtable.org/news-center/business-groups-letter-opposing-china-currency-legislation.

H.R. 639/S. 328

H.R. 639 (Sander Levin) and S. 328 (Sherrod Brown), Currency Reform for Fair Trade Act, were introduced on February 14, 2011. The bills are nearly identical to the version of H.R. 2378 that passed in the House during the 111th Congress.[29] The bills seek to clarify certain provisions of U.S. countervailing duty laws (pertaining to foreign government export subsidies) that would allow the Commerce Department to consider a "fundamentally misaligned currency" as an actionable subsidy.[30] For example, they would clarify that a fundamentally undervalued currency could be treated by Commerce as a benefit conferred by a foreign government to its exports.[31] In addition, the bills seeks to clarify that, in the case of a subsidy relating to a fundamentally undervalued currency, the fact that the subsidy (i.e., the undervalued currency) may have also benefitted non-exporting firms (in addition to exporting firms), would not, for that reason alone, mean that the undervalued was not an actionable subsidy under U.S. countervailing duty law.[32] The bills would direct the Commerce Department to use, if possible, data and methodologies utilized by the International Monetary Fund (IMF) to estimate real effective exchange rate undervaluation.

Factors that would be used by the Commerce Department to determine if a country's currency is fundamentally undervalued for the purposes of U.S. countervailing duty laws would include (over an 18-month period): (1) protracted and large-scale intervention in currency markets; (2) a real effective exchange rate estimated to be undervalued by at least 5%; and (3) foreign asset reserves held by the government that exceed: (A) the amount needed to repay its debt obligations over the next year, (B) 20% of the nation's money supply, and (C) the value of the country's imports over the previous four months.

The bills direct the Commerce Department to estimate the "subsidy" relating to a fundamentally undervalued currency for the purpose of imposing countervailing duties, which would be defined as the difference between a currency's real effective exchange rate and its equilibrium real effective exchange rate.[33] The bill further directs Commerce (when appropriate) to use the simple average of the methodologies used by the IMF's Consultative Group on Exchange Rates. If such

---

[29] H.R. 639/S. 328 contain a provision that clarifies that provisions would also apply to the goods of Canada and Mexico; this was not included in the House-passed version of H.R. 2378.

[30] A number of U.S. countervailing duty petitions have included claims that China's currency policy is an actionable subsidy under U.S. countervailing duty law. Some petitioners have argued that when Chinese exporters are paid in dollars and subsequently exchange those dollars for Chinese RMB, the payment (RMB) they receive is larger than would occur under market conditions because of the Chinese government's intervention to keep the RMB artificially low against dollar. This policy is viewed as constituting a financial contribution or price support. The Commerce Department has yet to include an undervalued currency as part of its countervailing duty investigation. In one case involving imported aluminum extrusions from China, which included a charge by petitioners that China's undervalued currency was a countervailable subsidy, the Commerce Department stated that additional study of the issue was needed, given the unique nature of the alleged subsidy and the complex methodological issues that it raises under U.S. countervailing duty law. See for example, Department of Commerce, International Trade Administration, *Aluminum Extrusions from the People's Republic of China: Initiation of Countervailing Duty Investigation*, Federal Register, Volume 75, Number 80, April 27, 2010, p. 22117.

[31] The benefit would be defined as the difference between the amount of foreign currency received by the exporter from the transaction and the amount that would have been received if the currency was not undervalued.

[32] In other words, the undervalued currency could be considered to be a measure that is contingent upon export performance.

[33] Real effective exchange rates are defined as a weighted average of bilateral exchange rates, adjusted for inflation.

---

data are not available from the IMF, Commerce would be directed to use generally accepted economic and econometric techniques and methodologies to measure the level of undervaluation.

S. 1619

S. 1619 (Sherrod Brown), Currency Exchange Rate Oversight Reform Act of 2011, was introduced on September 22, 2011, and was passed by the Senate on October 11, 2011. The bill would provide for the identification of fundamentally misaligned currencies and require action to correct the misalignment for certain "priority" countries. The bill would require the Treasury Department to issue a semiannual report to Congress on international monetary policy and currency exchange rates, which, in addition to several provisions under current law,[34] would include:

- a description of any currency intervention by the United States or other major economies or trading partners of the United States, or other actions undertaken to adjust the actual exchange rate relative to the U.S. dollar;

- an evaluation of the domestic and global factors that underlie the conditions in the currency markets;

- with respect to currencies of countries with significant trade flows with the United States and other major global currencies, a determination and designation by Treasury as to which of these are in fundamental misalignment;

- a list of currencies designated for "priority action;"

- an identification of the nominal value associated with the medium-term equilibrium exchange rate relative to the U.S. dollar for each currency listed for priority action; and

- a description of any consultations conducted, including any actions taken to eliminate the fundamental misalignment.

Treasury would be required to seek negotiations with countries designated for priority action. Factors used to determine priority countries would include those that are: (1) engaging in protracted large-scale intervention in currency markets, particularly if accompanied by sterilization measures; (2) engaging in excessive and prolonged accumulation of foreign exchange reserves for balance of payment (BOP) purposes; (3) introducing or modifying restrictions or incentives (for balance of payment purposes) on capital inflows and outflows that are inconsistent with the goal of achieving full currency convertibility; and (4) pursuing any other policy or action that the Treasury Secretary views as warranting designation for priority action.

If a country that has a currency designated for priority action fails to eliminate the fundamental misalignment within 90 days, the following would occur:

- In antidumping duty investigations, the Commerce Department would be required to factor in the estimated level of currency undervaluation when comparing the export price with the normal value (i.e., the exporter's home market value) when determining the level of dumping that may have taken place.

---

[34] See §3004 of Omnibus Trade and Competitiveness Act of 1988 (22 U.S.C 5305).

- The President would be required to prohibit the procurement by the federal government of products or services from the country unless it is a party to the World Trade Organization's (WTO) Government Procurement Agreement (GPA). Although China is negotiating to join the GPA, it is currently not a member.

- The Overseas Private Investment Corporation (OPIC) would be prohibited from approving any new financing (including insurance, reinsurance, or guarantee) with respect to a project located within the country. This provision would not affect China because OPIC is already prohibited by U.S. law from operating in China.

- The U.S. Executive Director at each multilateral bank would be directed to oppose the approval of any new financing to the government of a country, or for a project located within that country.

- The United States would request the IMF to hold special consultations with the country on ways to eliminate the fundamental misalignment.

If a country that has a currency designated for priority action fails to take steps to eliminate the fundamental misalignment within 360 days after its designation by Treasury, the following would occur:

- The U.S. Trade Representative would be required to request consultations in the WTO with the country regarding the consistency of the country's actions with its obligations in the WTO.

- The Treasury Secretary would be required to consult with the Board of Governors of the Federal Reserve System to consider undertaking remedial intervention in international currency markets in response to the fundamental misalignment of the designated and coordinating such intervention with other monetary authorities and the IMF.

S. 1619 would also amend U.S. countervailing duty law to require the Commerce Department to initiate an investigation to determine whether currency undervaluation is providing, directly or indirectly, a countervailing subsidy if a petition is filed by an interested party and is accompanied by information supporting those allegations. The bill also seeks to clarify that, in the case of a subsidy relating to a fundamentally undervalued currency, the fact that the subsidy (i.e., the undervalued currency) may have also benefitted non-exporting firms would not, for that reason alone, mean that the subsidy could not be considered to be a measure that is contingent upon export performance. The bill includes waiver provisions for actions taken toward priority countries and a process for Congress to disapprove the waivers. S. 1619 would also add a provision to U.S. antidumping law that would require the Commerce Department to include whether a country has been designated as having a currency for priority action as a factor to be considered during a review of whether to change the designation of a non-market economy country to one that is a market economy country.[35]

---

[35] Under U.S. antidumping proceedings regarding imports from a non-market economy country (such as China), the Commerce Department may determine that the normal value of the product in question cannot be determined. In such cases, Commerce uses price information from "surrogate countries" that have a market economy to determine the normal value of the imported products in question. Some analysts contend that this practice results in higher antidumping rates on imports from nonmarket economy countries than on those from market economy countries.

For the purposes of measuring a benefit conferred by a misaligned currency in a regular countervailing duty case, Commerce would be directed to compare the simple average of the real exchange rates derived from the application of the IMF's equilibrium real exchange rate approach and the macroeconomic balance approach to the official daily exchange rate, relying on IMF or World Bank data, if available, or other international organizations or national governments if such data are not available. For a countervailing duty case involving a fundamentally misaligned currency for priority action, S. 1619 would direct Commerce to calculate the benefit of a misaligned currency by comparing the nominal value associated with the medium-term equilibrium exchange rate of the currency of the exporting country to the official daily exchange rate. For the purposes of antidumping duty cases involving a fundamentally misaligned currency for priority action, S. 1619 would require the Department of Commerce to adjust the price used to establish the export price or constructed export price to reflect the fundamental misalignment of the currency of the exporting country. Fundamental misalignment is defined as a significant and sustained undervaluation of the prevailing real effective exchange rate, adjusted for cyclical and transitory factors, from its medium-term equilibrium level. The term "fundamental misalignment" and measurements of misalignment in H.R. 639/S. 328 and S. 1619 appear to have been largely drawn from the IMF's 2007 Decision on Bilateral Surveillance over Members' Policies (see text box below).

The IMF and Currency Misalignment

The IMF's 2007 Decision on Bilateral Surveillance over Members' Policies set new guidelines on exchange rate policies and identified certain developments that could affect global external stability, including exchange rate policies which in turn could trigger a thorough review by the IMF and possible consultations with an IMF member. Developments that could trigger a review include: (1) protracted large-scale intervention in exchange markets; (2) official or quasi-official borrowing that is unsustainable or brings unduly high liquidity risks or excessive and prolonged accumulation of foreign assets for balance of payment purposes; (3) monetary and other financial policies that provide abnormal encouragement or discouragement to capital flows; (4) significant policies that restrict or provide incentives for capital flows or current transactions or payments; (5) large and prolonged current account deficits or surpluses; (6) large external sector vulnerabilities; and (7) fundamental exchange rate misalignment.

A fundamental exchange rate misalignment may trigger IMF review when: (1) there is a misalignment between the prevailing real effective exchange rate and the level that would bring the underlying current account in line with the equilibrium current account; (2) the misalignment is significant; (3) the significant misalignment is expected to persist under established exchange rate policies; and (4) the significant and persistent misalignment is established beyond any reasonable doubt. The equilibrium real effective exchange rate is defined as one that is consistent with an underlying current account (adjusted for temporary factors) that is estimated to be in line with economic fundamentals, (such as productivity differentials, the terms of trade, permanent shifts in factor endowments, demographics, and world interest rates), over the medium-term.[36]

S. 1130

S. 1130 and S. 1267 (John Rockefeller) would, among other things, treat "exchange rate manipulation" as an actionable subsidy under U.S. countervailing duty cases. Exchange rate manipulation would be defined as protracted large-scale intervention by a country to undervalue the country's currency in the exchange market that prevents effective balance-of-payments adjustment or that gains an unfair competitive advantage over any other country.

---

[36] IMF, *Challenges to the International Monetary System: Rebalancing Currencies, Institutions, and Rates, Presentation by Mr. Takatoshi Kato*, September 30, 2011.

S. 1238

S. 1238 (Olympia Snowe) would require that, before Congress approves any bill implementing a free trade agreement or extending permanent normal trade relations status to another country, the President would have to first certify that the government of the potential trading partner has not, in the ten years preceding the certification, manipulated its currency for the purposes of gaining an unfair advantage in international trade. In addition, the Senate would have to cease consideration of the trade agreement if a point of order was made by any Senator against the bill because it was not accompanied by the President's certification.[37]

The Obama Administration's Position and Policies

President Obama stated in February 2010 that China's undervalued currency puts U.S. firms at a "huge competitive disadvantage," and he pledged to make addressing China's currency policy a top priority.[38] At a news conference in November 2011, President Obama stated that China needed to "go ahead and move towards a market-based system for their currency" and that the United States and other countries felt that "enough is enough."[39]

Administration officials have welcomed greater congressional involvement on the China currency issue as long as legislative proposals do not violate U.S. WTO obligations and do not complicate ongoing bilateral and multilateral negotiations with China on the issue. The Administration did not publicly indicate whether it supported or opposed the House-passed version of H.R. 2378 in the 111th Congress. During considering of S. 1619 by the Senate in October 2011, an Administration official stated that "we share the goal of the legislation in taking action to ensure that our workers and companies have a more level playing field with China, including addressing the under-valuation of their currency, an issue that I've spoken about and certainly Secretary Geithner and others have spoken about. Aspects of the legislation do, as I've said, raise concerns about consistency with our international obligations, which is why we're in the process of discussing with Congress those issues. And if this legislation were to advance, we would expect those concerns to be addressed."[40]

The Obama Administration has sought to directly engage China on the currency issue through the Strategic & Economic Dialogue (S&ED) and the Joint Commission on Commerce and Trade (JCCT).[41] At the end of the May 2011 S&ED session, Secretary of the Treasury Tim Geithner stated: "We hope that China moves to allow the exchange rate to appreciate more rapidly and more broadly against the currencies of all its trading partners. And this adjustment, of course, is critical not just to China's ongoing efforts to contain inflationary pressures and to manage the

---

[37] The sponsors of the bill contend that China's undervalued currency policy "incentivizes other nations to follow its model as a way for their exporters to stay competitive with low-priced Chinese products" and that the bill was "intended to send the message that a key precondition to entering into any trade agreement with the U.S. should be the clear absence of any governmental currency intervention or manipulation." Source: Senator Olympia Snowe, *Press Release*, June 21, 2011.

[38] The White House, *Remarks by the President at the Senate Democratic Policy Committee Issues Conference*, February 3, 2010.

[39] The White House, *News Conference by President Obama*, November 14, 2011.

[40] The White House, *Press Briefing by Press Secretary Jay Carney*, October 12, 2011.

[41] China's currency issue was also a major topic under the U.S.-China Strategic Economic Dialogue (SED) that was started under the Bush Administration in 2006.

---

risks that capital inflows bring to credit and asset markets, but also to encourage this broad shift to a growth strategy led by domestic demand."[42]

It addition, it has sought to use multilateral channels, such as the Group of 20 (G-20) of leading economies and the IMF, as a means to boost international cooperation on external balances and exchange rate policies and to bring more pressure on China to appreciate its currency.[43] For example, on October 20, 2010, Secretary Geithner issued a proposal aimed at the G-20 meeting of finance ministers and central bank governors on October 23, 2010. The proposal contained three main points:[44]

- G-20 countries should commit to taking steps to reduce external imbalances (both surpluses and deficits) below a specified share of GDP over the next few years.

- G-20 countries should commit to refrain from exchange rate policies designed to achieve competitive advantage by either weakening their currency or preventing appreciation of an undervalued currency. G-20 emerging market countries with significantly undervalued currencies (and adequate precautionary foreign exchange reserves) need to allow their exchange rates to adjust fully over time to levels consistent with economic fundamentals. G-20 advanced economies should work to ensure against excessive volatility and disorderly movements in exchange rates.

- The G-20 should call on the IMF to assume a special role in monitoring progress on these commitments and should publish a semiannual report assessing progress the G-20 countries have made to achieve these goals.

China and a number of other G-20 members, though supporting efforts to rebalance the global economy, opposed the idea of using numerical targets.

An Economic Analysis of the Effects of China's Currency on the U.S. Economy

This section examines a number of issues pertaining to the effects of China's undervalued currency on the U.S. economy. The economic effects on the Chinese economy of an undervalued currency are examined later in the report.

---

[42] U.S. Department of State, *Joint Closing Remarks for the Strategic and Economic Dialogue,* May 10, 2011, available at http://www.state.gov/secretary/rm/2011/05/162969 htm.

[43] The multilateral approach may also act as an inducement for China to reform its currency policies. If other economies (especially Asia) agree not to intervene in currency markets to prevent their currencies from appreciating (or depreciate them to gain a competitive edge against Chinese exporters), China might agree to quicken the pace of currency appreciation and reform. If China went ahead and appreciated its currency, other Asian economies might do the same. This might help minimize Chinese concerns that an appreciating currency would disrupt its export sector.

[44] Department of Treasury, *Dear G-20 Colleagues letter*, October 20, 2010.

Is the RMB Undervalued, and If So, by How Much?

Given the rapid increase of China's exports and FDI inflows from 1994 (when the dollar peg was established) through the present time, one would have expected China's currency to have appreciated against the currencies of its major economic and trading partners, including the United States, had the RMB exchange rate been determined solely by market forces. To prevent appreciation, China has accumulated official foreign reserves equal to $2.5 trillion. The IMF over the past few years has stated that the RMB is undervalued, but in February 2010, it stated that the RMB was "assessed to be substantially undervalued from a medium-term perspective."[45]

There are numerous estimates of the RMB's undervaluation against the dollar, although the results vary widely depending on the methodologies and various assumptions used.[46] Relatively recent estimates of the RMB's undervaluation (and the year the estimate was made) include

- 12% (December 2009) by Helmut Reisen with the Organization of Economic Cooperation and Development;[47]

- 25% (December 2009) by Dani Rodrik of Harvard University;[48]

- 30% (April 2010) by Arvind Subramanian at the Peterson Institute for International Economics;[49]

- 40.2% (January 2010),[50] 24.2% (June 2010),[51] 28.4% (April 2011),[52] and 23.5% (November 2011)[53] by William R. Cline and John Williamson at the Peterson Institute for International Economics; and

- 50% (October 2009) by Niall Ferguson (Harvard University) and Moritz Schularick (Free University of Berlin).[54]

---

[45] IMF, Meetings of G-20 Deputies, Seoul, Korea, *Global Economic Prospects and Policy Challenges*, February 27, 2010.

[46] For a survey of methodologies used to estimate a currency's true value, see CRS Report RL32165, *China's Currency: Economic Issues and Options for U.S. Trade Policy*, by Wayne M. Morrison and Marc Labonte.

[47] Reisen, Helmut, *On the Renminbi and Economic Convergence*, December 17, 2009. Available at http://www.voxeu.org/index.php?q=node/4397.

[48] Rodrick, Dani, *Making Room for China in the World Economic*, December 17, 2009. Available at http://www.voxeu.org/index.php?q=node/4399.

[49] Subramani, Arvind, *New PPP-Based Estimates of Renminbi Undervaluation and Policy Implications*, Peterson Institute For International Economics Policy Brief, number PB10-8, April 2010. Available at http://www.iie.com/publications/pb/pb10-08.pdf.

[50] Cline, William R. and John Williamson, *Notes on Equilibrium Exchange Rates*, Peterson Institute for International Economics, Policy Brief PB10-2, January 2010, available at http://www.iie.com/publications/interstitial.cfm?ResearchID=1472.

[51] Cline, William R. and John Williamson, Peterson Institute for International Economics, *Estimates of Fundamental Equilibrium Exchange Rates, May 2010*, Policy Brief 10-15, June 2010. Available at http://www.petersoninstitute.org/publications/interstitial.cfm?ResearchID=1596.

[52] Cline, William R. and John Williamson, Peterson Institute for International Economics, *Estimates of Fundamental Equilibrium Exchange Rates, May 2011*, Policy Brief 11-5. Available at http://www.iie.com/publications/interstitial.cfm?ResearchID=1841.

[53] Cline, William R. and John Williamson, Peterson Institute for International Economics, The Current Currency Situation, Number PB11-18, November 2011, at http://www.piie.com/publications/pb/pb11-18.pdf.

[54] Harvard Business School, *The End of Chimarica*, by Niall Ferguson and Moritz Schularick, Working Paper 10-937, October 2009. Available at http://www.hbs.edu/research/pdf/10-037.pdf.

Why Do Estimates of the RMB's Undervaluation Differ so Much?

Two main methods are used in the estimates presented above. One method is referred to as the fundamental equilibrium exchange rate (FEER) method. It is based on the belief that current account balances around the world are temporarily out of line with their "fundamental" value. Once an estimate has been made of what the fundamental current account balance should be, one can calculate how much the exchange rate must change in value to achieve that current account adjustment. To calculate the level of misevaluation for one country under this method, estimates of how far exchange rates for every country are out of equilibrium, including countries with floating exchange rates, must be made.

The main source of contention in FEER estimates is choosing an "equilibrium" current account balance for each country. Estimates of the RMB's undervaluation are typically defined as the appreciation that would be required for China to attain "equilibrium" in its current account balance. But there is no consensus based on theory or evidence to determine what equilibrium would be, so a subjective opinion is used.[55] Yet this assumption is crucial—Dunaway et al. demonstrate that changing the assumed equilibrium current account balance by 2 percentage points of GDP changes the estimated undervaluation by as much as 25 percentage points.[56] Some economists argue that the current account balance would always be close to zero in equilibrium, but this neglects the fact that countries with different saving and investment rates may willingly and profitably lend to and borrow from one another for long periods of time. If one uses China's neighbors as a reference point, the same combination of large foreign exchange reserves and a large current account surplus can be seen in several other countries in the region, even though these countries range in their exchange rate regimes from a float (Japan and South Korea) to a currency board (Hong Kong). Wang argues that, based on estimates derived from other developing economies, China's equilibrium current account surplus may be even larger than the actual surplus, implying by the FEER method that the RMB is overvalued.[57]

The other method for estimating the RMB's undervaluation is based on the theory of purchasing power parity (PPP)—the theory that the same good should have the same price in two different countries. If it did not, then arbitrageurs could buy it in the less expensive country and sell it in the more expensive country until the price disparity disappeared. While PPP is a simple idea that is theoretically powerful, it has proven to be unreliable in reality: prices are consistently lower in developing countries than industrialized countries, for example. Some economists have tried to estimate what the RMB's value would be by attempting to control for predictable divergences from PPP. Still, these estimates should be considered with caution—even when sophisticated modifications have been made, PPP has been shown to help predict exchange rates only over the long run. Estimates based on PPP would identify any country's currency as overvalued or undervalued relative to the country to which it is being compared, regardless of whether the exchange rate is fixed or floating. Another drawback to the PPP approach is that the estimate will

---

[55] A thorough attempt to estimate exchange rates using this method can be found in John Williamson, ed., *Estimating Equilibrium Exchange Rates* (Washington, DC: Institute for International Economics, 1994).

[56] Steven Dunaway et al., "How Robust are Estimates of Equilibrium Real Exchange Rates: The Case of China," IMF working paper 06/220, October 2006.

[57] Tao Wang, "Exchange Rate Dynamics," in Eswar Prasad, ed., "China's Growth and Integration into the World Economy," International Monetary Fund, Occasional Paper 232, 2004, Ch. 4.

not tend to change much over time (if prices are relatively stable), even if the trade deficit is significantly changing.[58]

The Treasury Department's December 2006 report to Congress on exchange rates discusses the use of economic models and methodology to estimate a currency's "misalignment" or what the fair market rate exchange rate should be. The report noted that there is no single model that accurately explains exchange rate movements, that such models rarely, if ever, incorporate financial market flows, and that their conclusions can vary considerably, based on the variables used. However, the Treasury Department stated that examining such models can produce useful information in understanding exchange rate movements if they focus only on serious misalignments; use real effective, not bilateral, exchange rates; utilize several different models, recognizing that no one model will provide precise answers; focus only on protracted misalignments where currency adjustments are not taking place; supplement judgments about misalignment with analysis of empirical data, indicators, policies and institutional factors; and verify whether there are any market-based reasons for a currency's misalignment.[59]

The IMF's Consultative Group on Exchange Rates uses three different methodologies for its surveillance and assessment of the exchange rate regimes of its members, including an equilibrium real exchange rate (ERER) approach, an external sustainability (ES) approach, and the macroeconomic balance (MB) approach.[60] In July 2011, the IMF stated that it believed "that the renminbi remains substantially below the level consistent with medium-term fundaments." For the first time, the IMF made public its estimates of the RMBs undervaluation, which included 3% under the ERER approach, 17% under the ES approach, and 23% under the MB approach.[61]

However, an IMF report that described its three exchange rate methodologies cautioned:

> While adopting different empirical methodologies goes some way towards strengthening the robustness of exchange rate assessments, it should be recognized that such assessments are unavoidably subject to large margins of uncertainty. These relate to a number of factors, such as the potential instability of the underlying macroeconomic links, differences in these links across countries, significant measurement problems for some variables, as well as the imperfect "fit" of the models. Some of these problems may be more severe for emerging market economies, where structural change is more likely to play an important role and where limitations in terms of data availability and length of sample are more acute.[62]

The four different estimates of the RMB's undervaluation made by Cline and William in 2010 and 2011 illustrate the challenges posed by economic models. The authors note that they utilized

---

[58] William Cline and John Williamson, "Estimates of the Equilibrium Exchange Rate of the Renminbi," paper presented at the Conference on China's Exchange Rate Policy, Peterson Institute, October 12, 2007.

[59] U.S. Treasury Department, *Report on International Economic and Exchange Rate Policies*, December 2006, Appendix II.

[60] The ERER approach estimates an equilibrium real exchange rate for each country as a function of medium-term fundamentals, such as the net foreign asset (NFA) position of the country, relative productivity differential between the tradable and non-tradable sectors, and the terms of trade. The ES approach calculates the difference between the actual current account balance and the balance that would stabilize the NFA position of the country at some benchmark level. The MB approach calculates the difference between the current account balance projected over the medium term at prevailing exchange rates and an estimated equilibrium current account balance, or "CA norm." See International Monetary Fund, *Methodology for CGER Exchange Rate Assessments*, November 8, 2006.

[61] International Monetary Fund, *People's Republic of China, 2011 Article IV Consultation*, July 2011, p.18.

[62] International Monetary Fund, Methodology for CGER Exchange Rate Assessments, November 8, 2006, pp. 4-5.

---

different methods and assumptions for their studies, which attempt to determine fundamental equilibrium exchange rates (FEERs) for various currencies, including the RMB.[63] For example, they note that the economic data used for their estimates came from the IMF's World Economic Outlook on projections of future economic variables (such as GDP growth and current account balances). The first study used data from the IMF's October 2009 Outlook, the second used the IMF's April 2010 Outlook, the third and fourth studies used the IMF's April 2011 Outlook. Using different forecast data thus helped produce different results. In addition, Cline and Williamson make FEERs estimates for different time periods. For example, the May 2011 study estimated the FEER-consistent exchange rate of the RMB against the dollar for April 2011, while the November 2011 study estimated that figure for late October 2011.[64]

It is worth nothing that Cline and Williamson's analysis made FEER estimates relative to the dollar for a number of currencies, not just the RMB (while the other studies cited in this report focused only on the RMB). Cline and Williamson's November 2011 study looked at the currencies of 29 countries. They estimated that in late October 2011, the currencies of 26 countries were undervalued against the dollar, while three were overvalued. Countries with currencies that were estimated to be the most misaligned against the dollar using the FEER are listed in **Table 1**. Singapore, Taiwan, Malaysia, and Hong Kong were estimated to have currencies that were more undervalued against the dollar than the Chinese RMB.

Table 1. Estimates of Currency Misalignment Against the Dollar in October 2011 for Selected Countries Based on the FEER Method

(%)

Country	Estimated Percent Change in Exchange Rate Needed to Obtain an FEER-Consistent rate with the Dollar (%)
Singapore	37.4
Taiwan	32.2
Malaysia	31.0
Hong Kong	29.7
China	23.5
Indonesia	15.5
India	15.3
Sweden	15.0

Source: Cline, William R. and John Williamson, Peterson Institute for International Economics, The Current Currency Situation, Number PB11-18, November 2011.

---

[63] Cline and William define a FEER as "an exchange rate that is expected to be indefinitely sustainable on the basis of existing policies. It should therefore be one that is expected to generate a current account surplus or deficit that matches the country's underlying capital flow over the cycle, assuming that the country is pursuing internal balance as well as it can and that it is not restricting trade for balance-of-payments reasons." For China, the authors assume that the exchange rate should be one consistent with a Chinese current account surplus of no more than 3% of GDP. The authors also assume that the United States should not run a current account deficit of more than 3%.

[64] Cline and Williamson also estimated the real trade-weighted FEER of the RMB. Their analysis claimed that that the RMB was undervalued on a real trade-weighted basis by 10.6% in late October 2011 (compared to 16.0% in their estimate for April 2011.

Because there is no universally-accepted methodology for determining a country's real market exchange rate, the economic conditions that are used to determine "equilibrium" exchange rates change continuously, and since estimates of China's currency valuation differ so significantly, many analysts question their usefulness to U.S. policymakers in terms of providing a precise goal for an appreciation of the RMB or for use in trade remedy legislation that would seek to offset the benefit ("subsidy") conferred by the RMB's undervaluation, such as in U.S. anti-dumping and countervailing measures.

The Debate over the Effects of Exchange Rate Appreciation on Trade Flows and the Deficit

Many policymakers might expect that if China significantly appreciated its currency, U.S. exports to China would rise, imports from China would fall, and the U.S. trade deficit would decline within a relatively short period of time. For example, C. Fred Bergsten contends that a market-based RMB would lower the annual U.S. current account deficit by $100 billion to $150 billion.[65] But the issue of the possible effects of an RMB appreciation on the U.S. economy is complicated by the fact that there are short-term and long-term implications of RMB appreciation, and that exchange rates are but one of many factors that affect trade flows. Other factors affecting the bilateral trade balance are discussed below.

The Bilateral Trade Deficit Continued to Grow during the Previous Period of RMB Appreciation

To illustrate that exchange rates are only one factor that determine trade flows, one can look at the effect of the 21% RMB appreciation of the RMB to the dollar from July 2005 to July 2008 on U.S.-China trade flows. On the one hand, during this period U.S. imports from China increased by 39%, compared to a 92% increase from 2001 to 2004 (when the exchange rate remained constant).[66] On the other hand, U.S. exports to China during the 2005-2008 period did not grow as fast as during the 2001-2004 period (71% versus 81%).[67] Despite the RMB's appreciation from 2005 to 2008, the U.S. trade deficit with China still rose by 30.1% (although the overall U.S. current account deficit declined by nearly 6%).[68] The appreciation of the RMB appears to have had little effect on China's overall trade balance from 2005 to 2008. During this time, China's merchandise trade surplus increased from $102 billion to $297 billion, an increase of 191%, and China's current account surplus and accumulation of foreign exchange reserves both increased by 165% over this period.

---

[65] *Correcting the Chinese Exchange Rate: An Action Plan,* by C. Fred Bergsten, Peterson Institute for International Economics, Testimony before the Committee on Ways and Means, U.S. House of Representatives, March 24, 2010.

[66] Some analysts contend that U.S. imports from China grew rapidly from 2001-2004, and slowed from 2005 to 2008, not because of the appreciation of the RMB, but because of changes to U.S. consumer demand relating to macroeconomic conditions.

[67] Trade varied from year to year. In 2008, U.S. imports from China rose by 5.1% over the previous year, compared to import growth of 11.7% in 2007; however, U.S. exports over this period were up 9.5% in 2008 compared with an 18.1% rise in 2007.

[68] The current global economic slowdown led to a sharp reduction in U.S.-China trade in 2009; both U.S. exports to and imports from China fell sharply, though imports fell at a bigger rate. As a result, the U.S. trade deficit with China was down 14.8% over the previous year.

The J Curve Effect

Part of the problem in attempting to evaluate the effects of the RMB's appreciation is that it can take time (perhaps a few years) before changes in exchange rates are reflected in changes to prices of tradable goods and services, and, hence, result in changes to imports, exports, and trade balances. An appreciated RMB could actually worsen the U.S. trade deficit in the short-run if the volume (demand) of imports from China did not decline at the same rate that prices increased (the so-called J-Curve effect). It would take time for U.S. consumers of higher-priced Chinese products to find lower-priced (non-Chinese) products or other alternatives and thus reduce overall demand for Chinese imports.[69] In addition, there would be a lag time in terms of the effects of an appreciated RMB on prices of Chinese products, since prices for many exports are set several months ahead of time in contracts. If an appreciated currency lowered prices for U.S. products, it could take time for increased Chinese demand to be signaled to U.S. producers and exporters and for them to boost production to meet the new demand. Over time, one would expect the effects of currency appreciation to affect the flow of bilateral trade and, possibly, produce a decrease in the bilateral trade imbalance (although the size of the overall U.S. trade deficit might not change because that is determined by a number of factors other than exchange rates).

The Role of Exchange Rate Pass-Through

Another factor to consider in attempting to evaluate the effects of an RMB appreciation on trade flows is to examine how price changes would be passed on or distributed. If the RMB appreciates against the dollar, not all of the price increase resulting from the appreciation may be passed on to the U.S. consumer. Some of it may be absorbed by Chinese laborers, producers, or exporters, and some by U.S. importers, wholesalers, retailers, etc. According to the U.S. Department of Labor, from July 2005 to July 2008, the price index for U.S. imports from China rose by 5.2% (compared to a 13.2% rise in import prices for total U.S. imports of non-petroleum products).[70] This would suggest that very little of the price increase that might have resulted from the RMB's appreciation was passed on to U.S. consumers.[71] If prices are not completely passed through to consumers, then consumer demand for Chinese imports will fall less than if they were, all else equal.

China's Role in the Global Supply Chain

The issue of exchange rate effects is further complicated by China's role as a major assembly center for multinational corporations. Many analysts contend that the sharp increase in U.S. imports from China over the past several years (and hence the growing bilateral trade imbalance) is largely the result of movement in production facilities from other (primarily Asian) countries to China. That is, various products that used to be assembled in such places as Japan, Taiwan, Hong Kong, etc., and then exported to the United States are now being made in China (in many cases, by U.S. and other foreign firms in China) and exported to the United States. According to Chinese data, foreign-invested firms in China account for over half of China's trade flows (both exports

---

[69] Depending on the elasticity of demand for the product, some might be willing to pay the extra price and buy the same level as before, some might buy less of the product, and some might stop purchasing the product altogether.

[70] Bureau of Labor Statistics, *Import/Export Price Indexes*, Press Release, various issues.

[71] Some of the costs may have been borne by Chinese producers or workers. Alternatively, China might have been able to boost efficiency, thus lowering costs, or production could have moved inland where labor is less expensive.

and imports). Such firms import raw materials, intermediate goods (such as components), and production machinery to China. One study of Apple Inc.'s iPod found that the product itself was assembled in China in factories owned by a Taiwanese company from components that were produced by numerous multinational corporations. The level of value added by Chinese workers who assembled the iPod in China was estimated to be small relative to the total cost of producing each unit (about 3%), and much smaller relative to the retail price of the unit sold in the United States.[72] Some analysts contend that, because of the high level of imported inputs that comprise a large share of China's exports, an appreciated RMB would have little effect on the prices of Chinese exports, and hence have little effect on bilateral trade flows. Others contend that, even if foreign-invested firms in China faced significantly higher costs because of an appreciated RMB, they would move production to another low-cost country, and thus, while the U.S trade deficit with China decreased, the U.S. trade deficit with other countries would increase.

Underlying Macroeconomic Imbalances Are Unlikely to Disappear

By accounting identity, the overall trade deficit is equal to the shortfall between domestic saving and investment, while an overall trade surplus is equal to a surplus of domestic saving relative to investment. For many years, China has been a high-saving country that has run overall trade surpluses and the United States has been a low-saving country that has run overall trade deficits (for more discussion on this issue, see **Appendix**). China's use of an exchange rate peg and capital controls may have contributed to its high saving rate, but it is unlikely that movement to a floating exchange rate would eliminate the large disparity between U.S. and Chinese saving rates. Thus, it is likely that the United States would continue to be a net debtor and China would continue to be a net creditor if the RMB rose in value. If so, economic theory predicts the countries' bilateral trade imbalance would either persist or possibly be replaced by new bilateral imbalances with third countries.

Differing Opinions on Making RMB Appreciation a Top U.S. Trade Priority

As noted earlier, a number of U.S. economists have argued that China's undervalued currency has negatively affected the U.S. and global economies. However, other economists contend that, while an undervalued RMB may have distorted trade flows to some extent, it is not the most significant challenge to U.S. economic interests vis-à-vis China, and therefore, they argue, an appreciation of the currency by itself would do little to boost the U.S. economy. For example,

- Derek Scissors at the Heritage Foundation contends that appreciation of the RMB would have little impact on U.S. employment, stating it would create "a few thousand jobs at best."[73] He argues that the Chinese government's extensive use of industrial policies, namely subsidies and regulatory protection (such as state-sponsored monopolies) sharply limits imports of goods and services that compete with the state sector, which would remain unaffected even if the RMB was appreciated. He notes: "Guaranteed revenue and economies of scale make state firms modestly competitive as exporters when they would otherwise be uncompetitive. The real harm, however, is to imports of goods and services from

---

[72] Communications of the ACM, *Who Captures Value in a Global Innovation Network? The Case of Apple's iPod*, March 2009.

[73] He also argues that reducing the federal budget deficit in the long run is the best way to boost employment and states that "in comparative importance, the value of the RMB is a footnote."

the U.S. The degree of state predominance caps the total share available to all domestic private and foreign companies, leaving American producers in a vicious battle for permanently minor market segments. This is a far more stringent limitation than an undervalued currency."[74]

- Michael Pettis with the Carnegie Endowment for International Peace makes a similar argument except that he contends that Chinese government "financial repression" policies have kept real returns to deposits low (and sometimes negative) in China in order to keep real lending rates artificially low (since they are set by the government, not market conditions) for Chinese firms (especially state-owned firms). He states that this constitutes a forced transfer of income from Chinese households to Chinese producers, which has led to over-investment and over-capacity by Chinese firms, with much of that excess capacity being exported. Pettis concludes that "as long as China continues to subsidize its production growth at the expense of household income, it will have difficulty increasing domestic demand and cutting its reliance on exports."[75]

- A study by the Federal Reserve Bank of San Francisco contends that, although the United States is running record trade deficits with China, the level of imports from China relative to U.S. GDP and U.S. personal consumption expenditures is relatively small.[76] According to the study, U.S. imports of goods and services from China accounted for 2.5% of GDP in 2010, and these imports accounted for only 2.7% of U.S. personal expenditures for goods and services in 2010.[77] The study estimated that on average for every one dollar that is spent in the United States on a product that is labeled "made in China," 55 cents goes for services supplied in the United States, such as transportation, wholesale, and retail. As a result, according to the study, the actual value of goods and services originating in China totaled only 1.2% of U.S. personal expenditures in 2010; accounting for the level of imported intermediate inputs from China that are used to manufacture goods that are labeled "made in the USA" would raise this level to 1.9%. Some argue that the Federal Reserve Bank study illustrates that U.S. imports from China do not necessarily displace U.S. workers (and in fact, support U.S. jobs in a number of sectors) and that RMB appreciation would likely have little effect on the U.S. economy.

Winners and Losers of RMB Appreciation from an Economic Perspective

Economists generally oppose the use of polices (such as subsidies and trade protection) that interrupt market forces and distort the most efficient distribution of resources. A fixed or managed

---

[74] Heritage Foundation, WebMemo, *Deadlines and Delays: Chinese Revaluation Will Still Not Bring American Jobs*, April 6, 2010.

[75] Carnegie Endowment for International Peace, *How Can China Reduce Its Reliance on Net Exports?,* June 24, 2010.

[76] The Federal Reserve Bank of San Francisco Economic Letter, *The U.S. Content of "Made in China,"* August 8, 2011, at http://www.frbsf.org/publications/economics/letter/2011/el2011-25.html.

[77] According to the U.S. Bureau of Economic Analysis, personal consumption expenditures is the primary measure of consumer spending on goods and services in the U.S. economy, accounting for about two-thirds of domestic final spending, and thus it is the primary engine that drives future economic growth. See U.S. Bureau of Economic Analysis website at http://www.bea.gov/national/pdf/NIPAhandbookch5.pdf.

---

float exchange rate whose level is not adjusted when economic conditions change might be viewed as a such a distortion.[78] Thus, from an economist's perspective, adopting a more market-based currency would be a win-win situation for China, the United States, and the global economy as a whole, in the sense that it would lead to a more efficient allocation of resources in both countries (though not necessarily any effect on overall employment levels, as discussed below). From a policy perspective, it could be argued that China's current undervalued currency produces economic "winners and losers" in both countries, and therefore, an adjustment to that policy would produce a new set of economic "winners and losers." Although numerous factors affect global economic growth and trade flows, let us assume that an appreciation of the RMB produces a significant change in trade. What would the effects be for the U.S. economy?

Effect on U.S Exporters and Import-Competitors

When exchange rate policy causes the RMB to be less expensive than it would be if it were determined by supply and demand, it causes Chinese exports to be relatively inexpensive and U.S. exports to China to be relatively expensive. As a result, U.S. exports and the production of U.S. goods and services that compete with Chinese imports fall, in the short run.[79] Many of the affected firms are in the manufacturing sector.[80] This causes the trade deficit to rise and reduces aggregate demand in the short run, all else equal. A market-based exchange rate could boost U.S. exports and provide some relief to U.S. firms that directly compete with Chinese firms.

Effect on U.S. Consumers and Certain Producers

According to economic theory, a society's economic well-being is usually measured not by how much it can produce, but how much it can consume. An undervalued RMB that lowers the price of imports from China allows the United States to increase its consumption through an improvement in the terms-of-trade. Since changes in aggregate spending are only temporary, from a long-term perspective, the lasting effect of an undervalued RMB is to increase the purchasing power of U.S. consumers. Imports from China are not limited to consumption goods. U.S. firms also import capital equipment and inputs from China to produce finished goods. An undervalued RMB lowers the price of these U.S. products, increasing their output, and thus making such firms more internationally competitive. An appreciation of China's currency could raise prices for U.S. consumers, lowering their economic welfare, meaning they have less money to spend on other goods and services. In addition, firms that use imported Chinese parts could face higher costs, making them relatively less competitive.

---

[78] The standard economic model for determining whether countries should have a floating exchange rate is the "optimal currency area" model. According to this model, two countries can gain from fixed exchange rates if their goods and labor markets are highly interconnected and their business cycles are closely synchronized. By these criteria, China and the United States are unlikely to form an optimal currency area.

[79] Many such firms contend that China's currency policy constitutes one of several unfair trade advantages enjoyed by Chinese firms, including low wages, lack of enforcement of safety and environmental standards, selling below cost (dumping) and direct assistance from the Chinese government.

[80] U.S. employment in manufacturing as a share of total non-agricultural employment fell from 31.8% in 1960, to 22.4% in 1980, to 13.1% in 2000, to 8.9% in 2010. This trend is much larger than the Chinese currency issue and is caused by numerous other factors, including productivity gains in manufacturing (such as through new technologies) and the rise of employment in the service sector.

Effect on U.S. Borrowers

An undervalued RMB also has an effect on U.S. borrowers. When the United States runs a current account deficit with China, an equivalent amount of capital flows from China to the United States, as can be seen in the U.S. balance of payments accounts. This occurs because the Chinese central bank or private Chinese citizens are investing in U.S. assets, which allows more U.S. capital investment in plant and equipment to take place than would otherwise occur. Capital investment increases because the greater demand for U.S. assets puts downward pressure on U.S. interest rates, and firms are now willing to make investments that were previously unprofitable. This increases aggregate spending in the short run, all else equal, and also increases the size of the economy in the long run by increasing the capital stock. The effect on interest rates is likely to be greater during periods of robust economic growth, when investment demand is strong, than when the economy is weak.

Private firms are not the only beneficiaries of the lower interest rates caused by the capital inflow (trade deficit) from China. Interest-sensitive household spending, on goods such as consumer durables and housing, is also higher than it would be if capital from China did not flow into the United States. In addition, a large proportion of the U.S. assets bought by the Chinese, particularly by the central bank, are U.S. Treasury securities, which fund U.S. federal budget deficits. According to the U.S. Treasury Department, China held at least $1.15 trillion billion in U.S. Treasury securities as of September 2011, making it the largest foreign holder of such securities and accounting for 24.6% of total foreign holdings.[81] The U.S. federal budget deficit has increased rapidly since FY2008, causing a sharp increase in the amount of Treasury securities that must be sold. While the Obama Administration has pushed China to appreciate its currency, it has also encouraged it to continue to purchase U.S. securities. Some analysts contend that, although an appreciation of China's currency could help boost U.S. exports to China, it could also lessen China's need to buy U.S. Treasury securities, which could push up U.S. interest rates. In the unlikely worst case scenario, if China stopped buying Treasury securities at a time when the U.S. budget deficit is unusually high, it could destabilize financial markets by throwing into doubt the U.S. government's ability to sustain its current fiscal policy.[82]

Net Effect on the U.S. Economy

In the medium run, according to economic theory, an undervalued RMB neither increases nor decreases aggregate demand in the United States. Rather, it leads to a compositional shift in U.S. production, away from U.S. exporters and import-competing firms toward the firms that benefit from Chinese capital flows. Thus, it is expected to have no medium- or long-run effect on aggregate U.S. employment or unemployment. As evidence, one can consider that since the 1980s, the U.S. trade deficit has tended to rise when unemployment was falling (and the economy

---

[81] The U.S. Treasury Department releases data on foreign holdings of U.S. securities on a monthly basis. Revisions to these data are often made annually. The revised data attempt to better reflect the country of origin of the purchaser, rather than the country from which the securities were purchased. Previous revisions by the Treasury Department of its data significantly increased the estimated level of China's holdings of U.S. securities. Thus China's holdings of U.S. securities as of September 2011 are likely much larger than $1.15 trillion.

[82] China has expressed concern in recent years over the "safety" of its large holdings of U.S. debt. It has criticized the U.S. Federal Reserve's easy monetary policies to boost economic growth, such as quantitative easing (involving large-scale purchases of U.S. Treasury Securities). Chinese officials claim that such policies could lead to a sharp devaluation of the dollar against global currencies and boost U.S. inflation, which could diminish the value of China's dollar holdings.

was growing) and fall when unemployment was rising (and the economy was slowing). For example, the U.S. current account deficit peaked at 6.0% of GDP in 2006, when the unemployment rate was 4.6%, and fell to 2.7% of GDP in 2009, when the unemployment rate was 9.3%.

However, the gains and losses in employment and production caused by the trade deficit will not be dispersed evenly across regions and sectors of the economy: on balance, some areas will gain while others will lose. And by shifting the composition of U.S. output to a higher capital base, the size of the economy would be larger in the long run as a result of the capital inflow/trade deficit (although the returns from foreign-financed capital will not flow to Americans).

Although the compositional shift in output has no negative effect on aggregate U.S. output and employment in the long run, there may be adverse short-run consequences. If U.S. output in the trade sector falls more quickly than the increases in output of U.S. recipients of Chinese capital, aggregate U.S. spending and employment could temporarily fall. This is more likely to be a concern if the economy is already sluggish than if it is at full employment. Otherwise, it is likely that government macroeconomic policy adjustment and market forces can compensate for any decline of output in the trade sector by expanding other elements of aggregate demand. The U.S. trade deficit with China (or with the world as a whole) has not prevented the U.S. economy from registering high rates of growth in the past.

A Yale University study estimated that a 25% appreciation of the RMB would initially decrease U.S. imports from China and lead to greater domestic production in the United States and increased exports to China. However, the study estimated that benefits to the U.S. economy would be offset by lower Chinese economic growth (because of falling exports), which would diminish its demand for imports, including those from the United States. In addition, the RMB appreciation would increase U.S. costs for imported products from China (decreasing real wealth and real wages), and cause higher U.S. short-term interest rates. As a result, the sum effect of the 25% RMB appreciation was estimated to a negative effect on U.S. aggregate demand and output and result in a loss of 57,100 U.S. jobs—less than one-tenth of 1% of total U.S. employment.[83]

Analysis by the IMF suggests that currency appreciation alone by China would yield limited benefits to the global economy (including the U.S. economy) unless it was accompanied by greater Chinese consumption and an expansion of the services sector. It estimated that a 20% RMB appreciation would boost U.S. economic growth by 0.05% to 0.07%, while a 20% RMB appreciation plus other reforms for rebalancing the Chinese economy would boost U.S. growth by over 0.15%.[84] The same study also estimated that a 20% RMB appreciation alone could reduce Chinese economic growth by 2.0% to 8.8%, while combining RMB appreciation with reforms for rebalancing could boost growth by up to 1%.[85]

---

[83] Fair, Ray C., "Estimated Macroeconomic Effects Of A Chinese Yuan Appreciation," Cowles Foundation Discussion Paper 1755, March 2010.

[84] International Monetary Fund, *People's Republic of China, 2011 Article IV Consultation,* July 2011, p. 36.

[85] On the other end of the IMF estimate, such scenario could slow China's growth by up to 2%.

China's Perspective and Concerns: Economic Growth and Stability

Chinese officials argue that their currency policy is not meant to favor exports over imports, but instead to foster economic stability through currency stability. The policy reflects the government's goals of using exports as a way of providing jobs to Chinese workers and to attract FDI in order to gain access to technology and know-how. The Chinese government has stated on a number of occasions that currency reform is a long-term goal which will be implemented gradually. Officials have strongly condemned international pressure to induce China to appreciate the currency, arguing that it interferes with China's "sovereignty" to implement its own domestic economic policies. In December 2009, China's media reported unnamed government officials as stating that "it would be difficult to make the case of an immediate renminbi appreciation in a country where 40 million people live on less than one U.S. dollar a day."[86] It also reported Chinese Premier Wen Jiabao stating that "some countries demand the yuan's appreciation, while practicing various trade protectionism against China. It's unfair and actually limits China's development."[87]

Despite the Chinese government's numerous pledges on currency reform, it has moved somewhat cautiously. Chinese officials view economic growth as critical to sustaining political stability, and thus appear very reluctant to implement policies that might disrupt the economy and cause widespread unemployment, which could cause worker unrest.[88] In addition, Chinese officials reject assertions by some economists that China's currency policy undermines the global economy or that a sharp appreciation of the RMB is needed to boost global economic recovery. Instead, they contend, that promoting rapid domestic growth is the most significant policy China can undertake to promote global economic recovery. They note that Chinese imports have risen rapidly in recent years, increasing by 38.8% in 2010 (over the previous year) and by 28.7% during the first 10 months of 2011 (year-on-year basis) (see **Figure 5**). Chinese officials contend that the rapid growth in imports proves that the currency policy does not restrict trade or promote Chinese economic growth at the expense of other countries. In addition, they note, China's merchandise trade surplus fell in 2009 and 2010, and, based on data for January-October 2011, will likely decline in 2011.[89] Critics counter that China's exports have grown rapidly since the beginning of 2009 and have surpassed pre-crisis levels, while China's real GDP growth over the past two years has been the highest (at 9.2% in 2009 and 10.3% in 2010) of any major economy. As a result, critics contend, China's efforts to hold down the value of its currency cannot be justified for economic reasons.

---

[86] *Xinhua News Agency*, December 1, 2009.

[87] Ibid.

[88] There have been numerous reports of labor unrest and strikes in different parts of China in 2010, mainly over pay issues. Chinese officials are concerned that an appreciation of the RMB could induce Chinese export producers to try to hold down wages to remain competitive, or could force them out of business, which could lead to more job losses and provoke more unrest.

[89] China's trade merchandise trade surplus fell from its peak of $297 billion in 2008 to $198 billion in 2009 and to $185 billion in 2010. China's trade surplus over the first 10 months of 2011 was down by 15.4% on a year-on-year basis, indicating that its trade surplus for the full year could total around $156 billion.

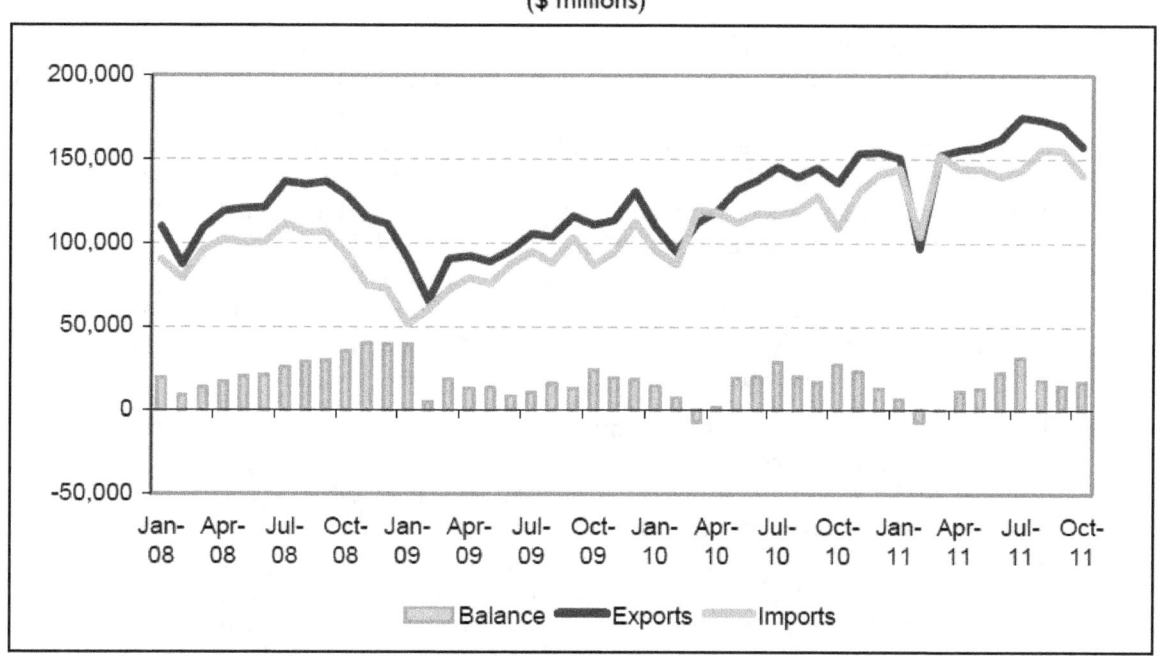

Figure 5. China's Monthly Trade Flows: January 2008-October 2011

($ millions)

Source: Global Trade Atlas using official Chinese statistics.

The Effects of an Undervalued RMB on China's Economy

If the RMB is undervalued vis-à-vis the dollar, then Chinese exports to the United States are likely less expensive than they would be if the currency were freely traded, providing a boost to China's export industries. Eliminating exchange rate risk through a managed peg also increases the attractiveness of China as a destination for foreign investment in export-oriented production facilities. However, there are a number of potentially negative aspects to China's export growth strategy and currency policy.

- Overdependence on exporting (and fixed investment relating to exports) and FDI inflows made China particularly vulnerable to the effects of the global economic slowdown. Analysis by the IMF estimated that fixed investment related to tradable goods plus net exports together accounted for over 60% of China's GDP growth from 2001 to 2008 (up from 40% from 1990 to 2000), which was significantly higher than in the G-7 countries (16%), the euro area (30%) and the rest of Asia (35%).[90]

- An undervalued currency makes imports more expensive, hurting Chinese firms that import parts, machinery, and raw materials. Such a policy, in effect, benefits Chinese exporting firms (many of which are owned by foreign multinational corporations) at the expense of non-exporting Chinese firms. This may impede the most efficient allocation of resources in the Chinese economy. Resources that

---

[90] Guo, Kai and Papa N'Diaye, *Is China's Export-Oriented Growth Sustainable*, IMF Working Paper, August 2009.

might go to other sectors, such as the service sector, are diverted to the export sector.

- If one considers an undervalued currency as a form of export subsidy, then China, in effect, is subsidizing American living standards by selling products that are less expensive than they would be under market conditions. This in effect lowers China's terms of trade—the level of imports that can be obtained through exports.[91] Chinese citizens on the other hand pay more for tradable goods, not only because imported goods are more expensive because of the de facto tariff an undervalued currency entails, but also because domestic competition is restricted as well. Rather than use its trade surpluses to purchase goods and services from abroad, China is forced, because of its need to maintain its peg to the dollar, to put a large share of its foreign exchange holdings into U.S. debt securities, which earn a relatively low return.

- The use of a pegged system greatly limits the ability of the central government to use monetary policy to control inflation, which has become a growing problem in China in 2011.[92] If Chinese banks raised interest rates in an effort to control inflation, overseas investors might to try to shift funds to China (through illegal means) to take advantage of the higher Chinese rates. The Chinese government has had difficulty blocking such inflows of "hot money." Such inflows force the government to boost the money supply to buy up the foreign currency necessary to maintain the targeted peg. Expanding the money supply contributes to easy credit policies by the banks, which has contributed to overcapacity in a number of sectors, such as steel, and speculative asset bubbles, such as in real estate.[93] In the past, the Chinese government has tried to use administrative controls, with limited results, to limit bank loans to sectors where overcapacity is believed to exist. In effect, a pegged currency induces the Chinese government to utilize inefficient and non-market financial policies for credit allocation, rather than a market-based system that would promote an efficient allocation of capital.

Although a rebalancing of China's economy, including the adoption of a market-based currency, would likely entail significant adjustment costs, it also would likely produce long-term benefits to the Chinese economy. For example it could:

- boost China's term of trade by increasing the level of imports that can be purchased by its exports;

- increase economic efficiency (and hence economic growth), by re-directing resources away from inefficient (and often subsidized) sectors of the economy to those that are more efficient and competitive;

---

[91] The ultimate goal of trade is to obtain imports in exchange for exports. The more imports a country can obtain from a given level of exports, the better off it is materially. China appears to be willing to "subsidize' its exports in order to boost jobs in export-oriented industries. However, Chinese consumers are made worse off.

[92] China's consumer price index in June 2011 rose by 6.4% over the same period in 2010, the largest jump in three years.

[93] The government can and has attempted to sterilize the increase of the money supply by forcing state banks to buy and hold government bonds.

- lower prices for imported goods and services and expose more of the domestic economy to greater global competition, thus lowering prices for consumers and improving Chinese living standards;

- improve the efficiency and competiveness of many Chinese domestic firms (including those that produce only for the domestic market) by lowering prices for imported inputs, raw materials, and machinery, thus boosting their output;

- expand the ability of the government to use monetary policies to control inflation and to allocate capital according to its most efficient use through a market-based credit system;

- help alleviate the large disparities of economic development between the coastal regions of China (as well as growing income disparities throughout China) that have been driven in part by China's export growth strategy and are viewed by many analysts as posing a potential risk to stability;

- help reduce or eliminate a major source of tension between China and many of its trading partners, some of whom view China's undervalued currency and its use of subsidies as beggar-thy-neighbor policies that promote economic development in China at the expense of growth in other countries.

The great challenge for Chinese leaders, assuming that they are committed to greater economic reform and rebalancing the economy, would be to quickly generate new sources of economic growth and job opportunities in order to offset the decline of those sectors that would no longer be able to compete once preferential government policies (such as subsidies and an undervalued currency) are eliminated. However, some analysts contend that this rebalancing could prove difficult for China politically and could take several years to achieve. For example, according to Michael Pettis, reforming China's economic policies would have to involve political reforms because "eliminating the mechanisms by which Chinese policymakers can transfer income from households to manufacturers will reduce their control over the commanding heights of the economy, and it will sharply reduce the power and leverage the ruling party has over business and local governments."[94] On the other hand, China's economy has consistently generated annual growth rates near 10% in recent decades, making adjustment much easier.

Policy Options for the RMB and Potential Outcomes

If the Chinese were to allow their currency to float, it would be determined by private actors in the market based on the supply and demand for Chinese goods and assets relative to U.S. goods and assets. If the RMB appreciated as a result, this would boost U.S. exports and the output of U.S. producers who compete with the Chinese. The U.S. bilateral trade deficit would likely decline (but not necessarily disappear). At the same time, the Chinese central bank would no longer purchase U.S. assets to maintain the peg. U.S. borrowers, including the federal government, would now need to find new lenders to finance their borrowing, and interest rates in the United States would rise. This would reduce spending on interest-sensitive purchases, such as capital investment, housing (residential investment), and consumer durables. The reduction in investment spending would reduce the long-run size of the U.S. capital stock, and thereby the

---

[94] Pettis, Michael, *Sharing the Pain: The Global Struggle Over Savings*, Carnegie Endowment for International Peace, November 2009, p. 7.

U.S. economy. In the present context of a large U.S. budget deficit, some analysts fear that a sudden decline in Chinese demand for U.S. assets (because China was no longer purchasing assets to influence the exchange rate) could lead to a drop in the value of the dollar that could potentially destabilize the U.S. economy.[95]

If the relative demand for Chinese goods and assets were to fall at some point in the future, the floating exchange rate would depreciate, and the effects would be reversed. Floating exchange rates fluctuate in value frequently and significantly.[96]

A move to a floating exchange rate is typically accompanied by the elimination of capital controls that limit a country's private citizens from freely purchasing and selling foreign currency. The Chinese government maintains capital controls (and arguably one of the major reasons China opposes a floating exchange rate) because it fears a large private capital outflow would result if such controls were removed. This might occur because Chinese citizens fear that their deposits in the potentially insolvent state banking system are unsafe. If the capital outflow were large enough, a banking crisis in China could result and could cause the floating exchange rate to depreciate rather than appreciate.[97] If this occurred, the output of U.S. exporters and import-competing firms would be reduced below the prevailing level, and the U.S. bilateral trade deficit would likely expand. In other words, the United States would still borrow heavily from China, but it would now be private citizens buying U.S. assets instead of the Chinese central bank. China could attempt to float its exchange rate while maintaining its capital controls, at least temporarily. This solution would eliminate the possibility that the currency would depreciate because of a private capital outflow. While this would be unusual, it might be possible. It would likely make it more difficult to impose effective capital controls, however, since the fluctuating currency would offer a much greater profit incentive for evasion.

Another possibility is for China to maintain the status quo. Even without adjustment to the nominal exchange rate, over time the real rate would adjust as inflation rates in the two countries diverged. The Chinese central bank acquires foreign reserves by printing yuan to finance its trade surplus. As the central bank exchanged newly printed yuan for U.S. assets, prices in China would rise along with the money supply until the real exchange rate was brought back into line with the market rate.[98] This would cause the U.S. bilateral trade deficit to decline and expand the output of U.S. exporters and import-competing firms. This real exchange rate adjustment would only occur over time, however, and pressures on the U.S. trade sector would persist in the meantime.

---

[95] For more information, see CRS Report R40770, *The Sustainability of the Federal Budget Deficit: Market Confidence and Economic Effects*, by Marc Labonte.

[96] Some economists argue that short-term movements in floating exchange rates cannot always be explained by economic fundamentals. If this were the case, then the floating exchange rate could become inexplicably overvalued (undervalued) at times, reducing (increasing) the output of U.S. exporters and U.S. firms that compete with Chinese imports. These economists often favor fixed or managed exchange rates to prevent these unexplainable fluctuations, which they argue are detrimental to U.S. economic well-being. Other economists argue that movements in floating exchange rates are rational, and therefore lead to economically efficient outcomes. They doubt that governments are better equipped to identify currency imbalances than market professionals.

[97] This argument is made in Morris Goldstein and Nicholas Lardy, "A Modest Proposal for China's Renminbi," *Financial Times*, August 26, 2003. Alternatively, if Chinese citizens proved unconcerned about keeping their wealth in Chinese assets, the removal of capital controls could lead to a greater inflow of foreign capital since foreigners would be less concerned about being unable to access their Chinese investments. This would cause the exchange rate to appreciate.

[98] To some extent, China can reduce the effects of the accumulation of foreign reserves on the money supply through credit controls, although this is unlikely to be completely effective.

None of the solutions guarantee that the bilateral trade deficit would be eliminated. China is a country with a high saving rate, and the United States is a country with a low saving rate; it is not surprising that their overall trade balances would be in surplus and deficit, respectively. As the **Appendix** discusses, many economists believe that these trade imbalances will persist as long as underlying macroeconomic imbalances persist. At the bilateral level, it is not unusual for two countries to run persistently imbalanced trade, even with a floating exchange rate. If China can continue its combination of low-cost labor and rapid productivity gains, which have been reducing export prices in yuan terms, its exports to the United States are likely to continue to grow regardless of the exchange rate regime, as evidenced by the 21% appreciation of the RMB from 2005 to 2008, which did not lead to any reduction in the trade deficit over that period.

Appendix. Indicators of U.S. and Chinese Economic Imbalances

The issue of rebalancing economic growth by both the United States and China has been a central focus of the U.S.-China Strategic and Economic Dialogue (S&ED) talks over the past two years. A joint statement issued at the May 2011 S&ED meeting noted that

> Since the second meeting of the Strategic and Economic Dialogue in May 2010, the economic recoveries in the United States and China have strengthened due to continued forceful stimulus measures undertaken by both countries, contributing to an improving outlook for the global economy. The two countries have also made progress on their commitments to promote more sustainable and balanced growth. To secure these gains and address potential challenges to the global outlook, we pledge to enhance macroeconomic cooperation to ensure that the global recovery is durable and promotes steady job growth, and to firmly establish strong, sustainable, and balanced growth.[99]

The global financial crisis and subsequent GDP decline among many countries have resulted in new scrutiny by many economists of "global imbalances," namely the disparities in savings and investment levels among various countries (i.e., some countries save too little and some too much relative to their investment needs), and subsequent current account imbalances that have resulted (i.e., countries where domestic savings exceed investment run trade surpluses, and countries where domestic investment exceeds saving run current account deficits). China and the United States are not unique in having these imbalances—Japan, Germany, and other East Asian countries are other examples of high savers, while southern and eastern European countries are other examples of high borrowers. Nevertheless, the United States and China have come under particular scrutiny because of their relative overall size (they are the world's two largest economies) and the relative size of their saving, investment, and trade imbalances. Some analysts also claim that China's exchange rate policy is preventing other East Asian countries from adjusting, because those countries are unwilling to allow their currencies to appreciate and lose export market share to China unless the RMB appreciates too.

Many economists contend such imbalances were a major cause of the current global economic slowdown. For example, high savers, such as China, loaned their money to low savers, such as the United States, which helped keep real U.S. interest rates low and contributed to the bubble in the U.S. housing market and subsequent financial crisis. Many of the high savings countries (especially those in Asia) heavily relied on exporting as a source of their economic growth and thus were significantly impacted when global demand for imports sharply fell.[100] As a result, many economists have called for economic restructuring among many of the world's major economies, especially the United States and China. Fundamental restructuring of this sort would take time, and if not well coordinated, could deepen the global output gap in the short run. For example, if low saving countries attempt to increase their saving rate (e.g., by reducing their government budget deficits) at a time of high unemployment, and high saving countries do not

---

[99] U.S. Department of the Treasury press release, Third Meeting of the U.S.-China Strategic & Economic Dialogue Joint U.S.-China Economic Track Fact Sheet, May 10, 2011. Available at http://www.treasury.gov/press-center/press-releases/Pages/tg1170.aspx.

[100] For an overview of this argument, see Blanchard, Olivier and Gian Maria Milesi-Ferretti, "Global Imbalances: In Midstream?" IMF Staff Position Note, December 22, 2009.

simultaneously increase their consumption, then worldwide demand could decline and cause unemployment to rise further in the short run.

This section provides an overview of some of the unique differences between the economies of the United States and China that have played a role in global imbalances.

Current Account Balances, Savings, and Investment

The level of U.S. gross savings is far below total U.S. investment, indicating that the United States must borrow capital abroad to meet its investment needs. By definition, domestic savings minus gross investment (from domestic and foreign sources) equals the current account balance.[101] Nations that do not save enough to meet domestic investment needs run current account deficits and those that save more than they need for domestic investment run current account surpluses.[102] In 2010, the ratio of U.S. gross domestic savings to gross investment was 74.3%, the lowest among the world's major economies. On the other hand, the ratio for China was 110.8% (see **Table A-1**).

In nominal dollar terms, the United States had the world's largest current account deficit in 2010 at $471 billion, while China had the largest current account surplus at $305 billion (see **Figure A-1**). These balances were also significant as a share of GDP: -3.2% for the United States and 5.2% for China (see **Figure A-2**).[103] Some "rebalancing" has taken place during the global recession. The U.S. current account deficit has declined from its peak 6.0% in 2006 because domestic investment spending has fallen and the private savings has risen.[104] On the other hand, this rebalancing has been partly offset by the increase in the U.S. budget deficit, which, as a percent of GDP rose from 1.2% in 2007 to 8.9% in 2010, which directly reduces national saving. What remains to be seen is how much of this rebalancing is cyclical, and will be reversed when the U.S. economy improves, and how much of it is permanent. China's current account surplus in 2010 was much smaller than it was at its peak of 10.6% in 2007.

Despite the rebalancing that has already taken place, some economists would not consider either country to have reached a position that is sustainable in the long run. Before the late 1990s, the United States had never had a current account deficit of 3% of GDP. And even with China's reduced current account surplus, and the diminished U.S. current account deficit over the past few years, China's net holdings of foreign assets and the U.S. net foreign debt continue to grow. Likewise, the decline in China's current account surplus was caused by a more rapid decline in China's exports than imports during the worldwide economic downturn—when worldwide growth picks up again and reaches pre-crisis levels, that trend could reverse.[105] As noted earlier,

---

[101] The current account balance is the broadest measurement of a country's financial flows. It includes the balances for trade in goods and services, net income (investment income and compensation for overseas workers), and net unilateral transfers.

[102] A current account deficit also reflects that a country consumes more than it produces, while a current account surplus indicates that a countries produces more than it consumes.

[103] The U.S. current account deficit as a percent of GDP fell in 2008 and 2009. China's current account surplus as a percent of GDP fell each year from 2007 to 2009.

[104] Gross private savings as a percent of GDP rose from 14.2% in 2007 to 18.2% in 2010. Source: Bureau of Economic Analysis.

[105] China's total trade during the first 10 months of 2011 have risen sharply, although imports have risen at a faster rate than exports, and it is projected that China's trade surplus for the full year will fall by 14.6% over the previous year. On the other hand, the U.S. trade deficit with China over the first 10 months of 2011 has risen by 8.2%.

---

the IMF projects China's current account balance as a percent of GDP will increase from 5.2% in 2011 to 7.2% in 2016, while the U.S. balance is projected to improve from -3.2% to -2.7%.

Table A-1. Ratio of Gross National Savings to Gross Investment and Current Account Balances as a Percent of GDP for Selected Major Economies: 2010

	Gross National Savings/Gross Investment (%)	Current Account Balance/GDP (%)
United States	**74.3**	**-3.2**
Italy	83.6	-3.3
France	89.2	-2.1
United Kingdom	83.2	-2.5
Brazil	88.2	-2.3
Canada	86.1	-3.1
India	90.5	-3.1
Mexico	97.8	-0.5
South Korea	109.5	2.8
Indonesia	102.7	0.9
China	**110.8**	**5.2**
Japan	117.7	3.6
Russia	121.0	4.8
Germany	132.3	5.7

Source: IMF.

Figure A-1. Chinese and U.S. Current Account Balances: 2000-2010

($ billions)

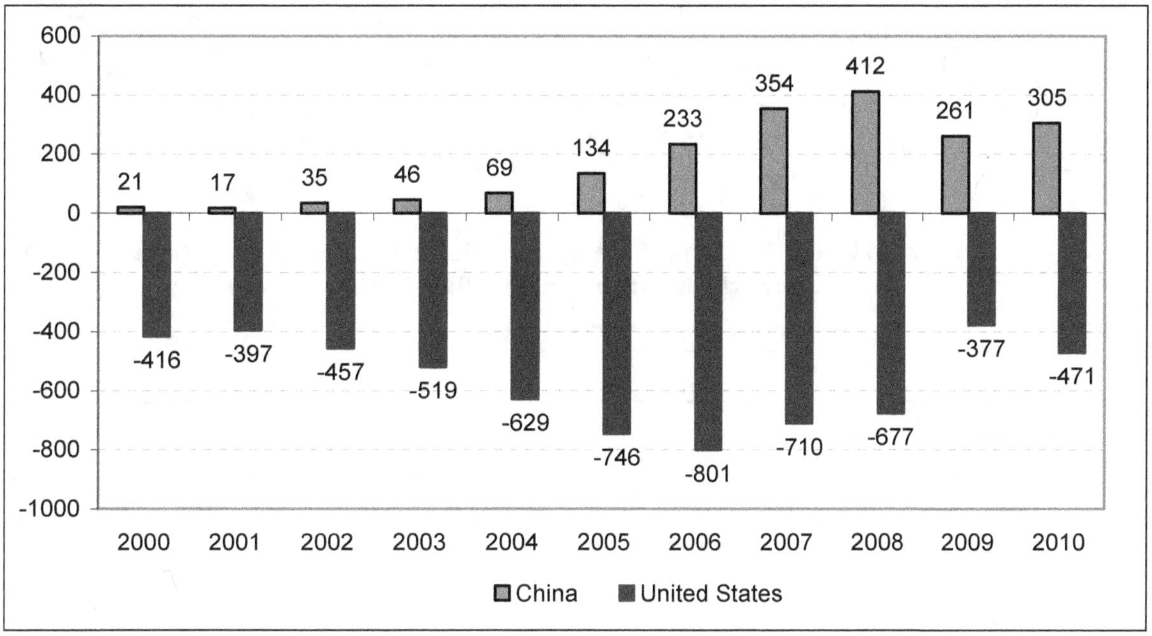

Source: IMF.

Figure A-2. Chinese and U.S. Current Account Balances as a Percent of GDP: 2000-2010

(percent)

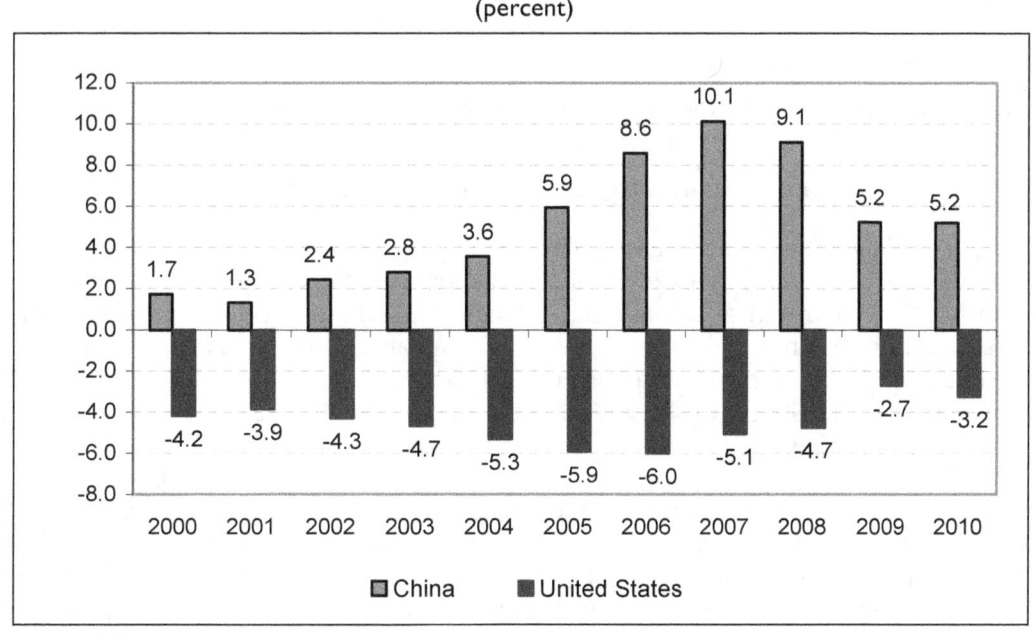

Source: IMF.

Gross savings are the total level of domestic savings, including private, corporate, and government. Savings represents income that is not consumed. Physical investment spending on plant and equipment can be financed from domestic or foreign savings. Over the past several years, the United States has maintained one of the lowest gross savings rates (i.e., total national savings as a percent of GDP) among developed countries, while China has maintained one of the world's highest national savings rates. From 1990 to 2010, U.S. gross national savings as a percent of GDP declined from 13.5% to 9.3%, while China's rose from 37.8% to 53.9% (see **Figure A-3**).

Figure A-3. Gross National Savings as a Percent of GDP for China and the United States: 1990-2010

(percent)

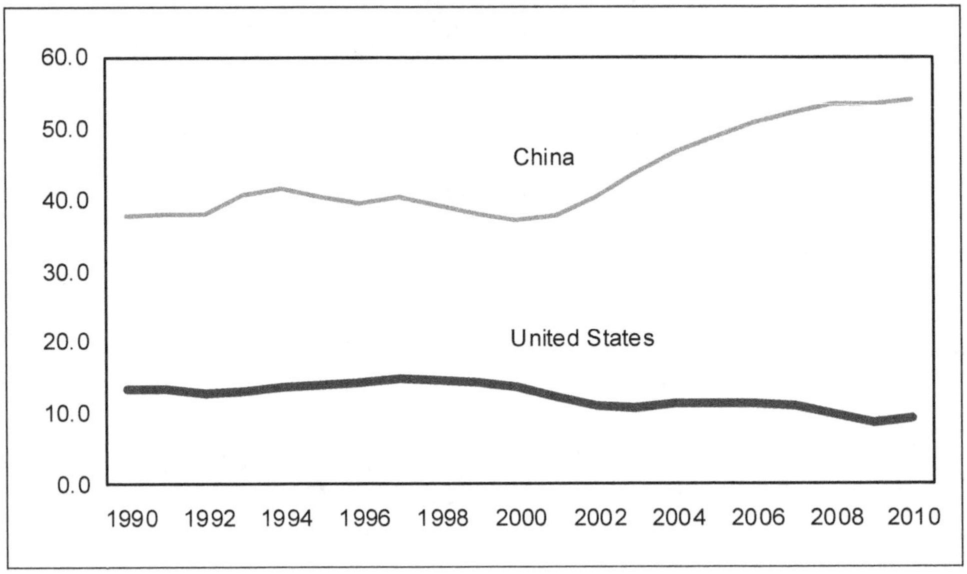

Source: Economist Intelligence Unit.

Notes: Aggregate national savings by the public and private sector as a percentage of nominal GDP.

Chinese Investment and Consumption Relative to GDP

As indicated in **Figure A-4**, China's gross investment as a percent of GDP in 2010 was the highest of any major economy at 46.2%, while, in comparison, the U.S. total was 12.0%, the lowest among the countries listed. Conversely, as indicated in **Figure A-5**, China had one of the lowest rates of private consumption as a share of GDP among major economies at 33.8%, while the U.S. rate was 70.6%—the highest among major economies. As indicated in **Figure A-6** the importance of gross investment to China's economy has increased sharply since 1990, while the importance of private consumption has fallen.

Although private consumption has been a much smaller share of China's GDP than other countries, the growth rate of China's private consumption has been significant. From 2000 to 2010, Chinese private consumption grew at an average annual rate of 7.8%, which was much faster than the growth in real U.S. private consumption, but slower than the overall growth rate of the Chinese economy (see **Figure A-7**).

Figure A-4. Gross Investment as a Percent of GDP for Selected Major Economies: 2010

(percent)

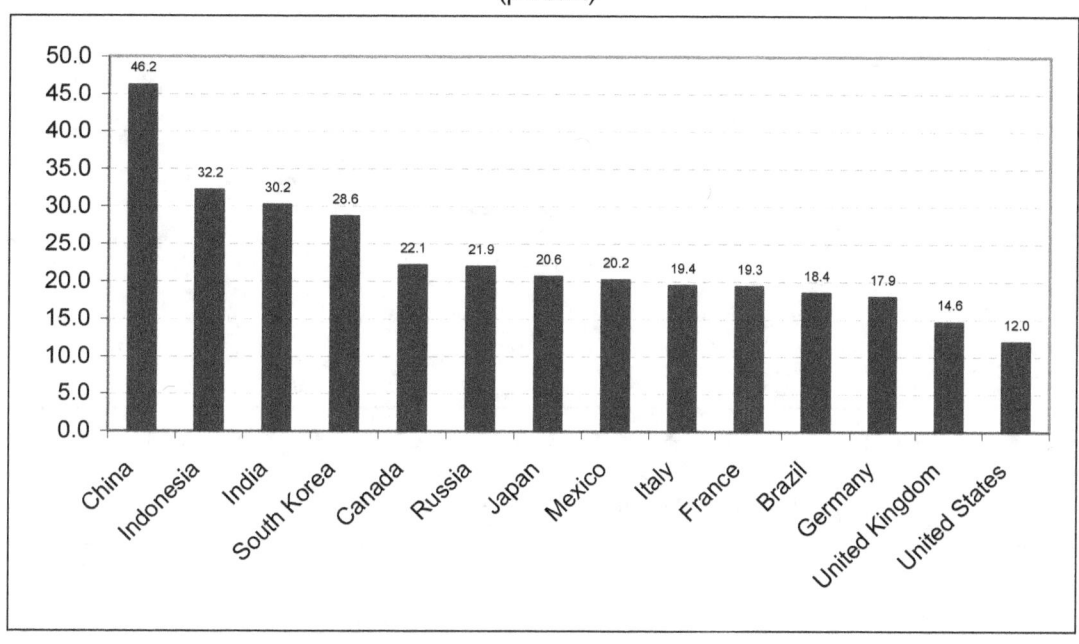

Source: Economist Intelligence Unit.

Figure A-5. Private Consumption as a Percent of GDP for Selected Economies: 2010

(percent)

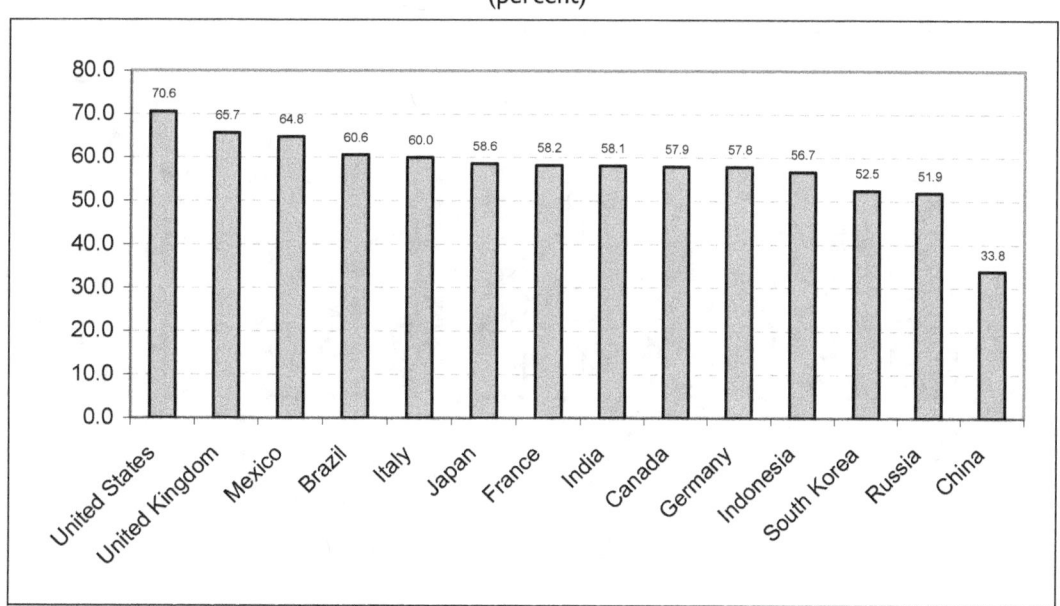

Source: Economist Intelligence Unit.

**Figure A-6. China's Gross Investment and Private Consumption as a Percent of GDP:
1990-2010**

(percent)

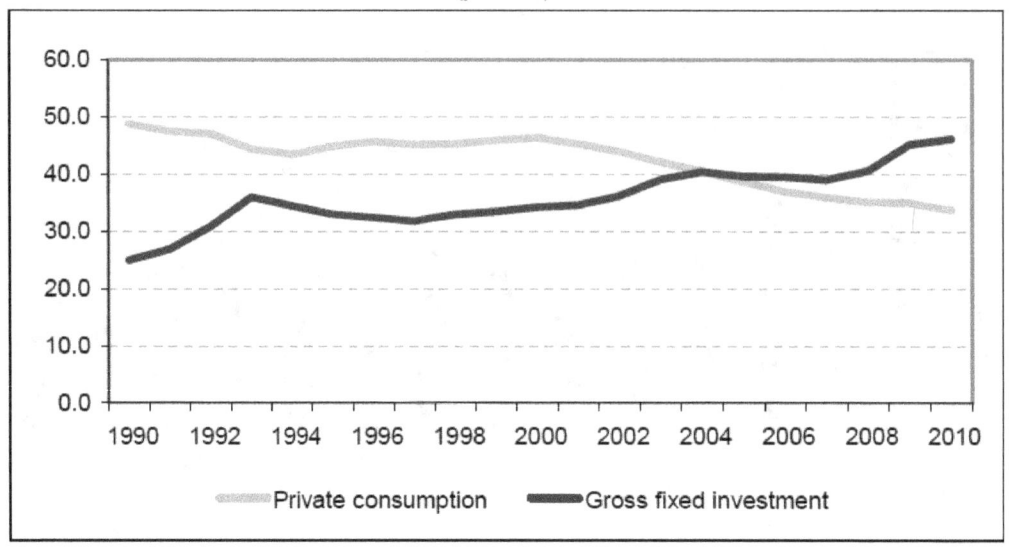

Source: EIU.

**Figure A-7. Annual Growth in Real Chinese and U.S. Private Consumption:
2000-2010**

(percent increase over the previous year)

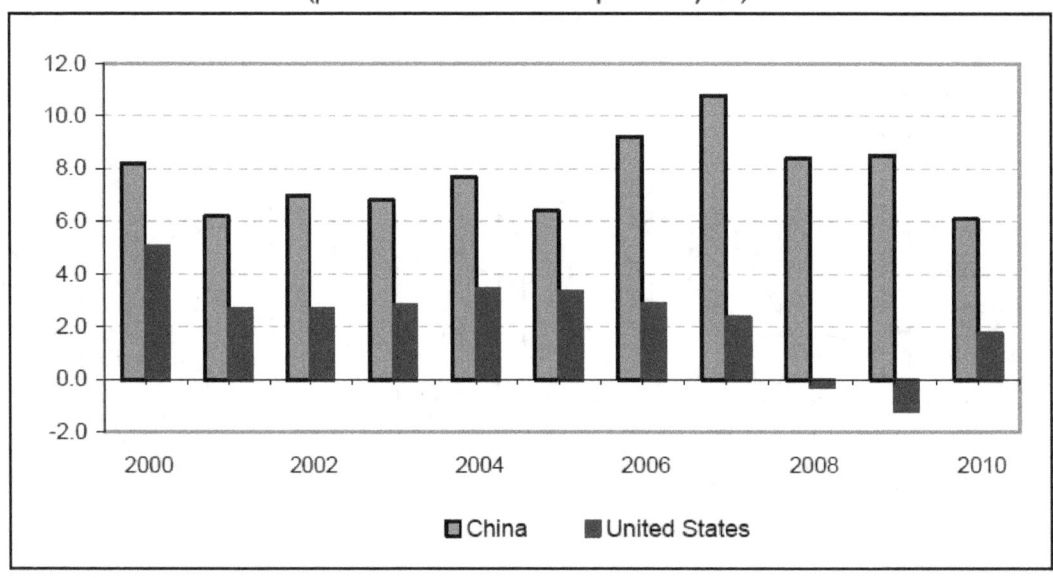

Source: Economist Intelligence Unit.

Many analysts contend that, although Chinese labor productivity has risen rapidly over the past several years, workers' wages have not kept pace with those productivity gains, largely due to the lack of worker rights in China, especially for migrant workers who tend to seek work in labor-intensive, export oriented, manufacturing. Rather, it is argued, the gains from productivity have largely accrued to Chinese firms. In addition, because the Chinese government maintains tight controls on capital outflows, Chinese households are limited in terms of where they can invest their savings. Most choose to deposit their savings in a Chinese bank. However, bank interest rates are set by the central government, and oftentimes, the rates of return on savings deposits are below the rate of inflation. Many economists contend that this policy represents an effort by the central government to keep the cost of credit low for Chinese firms (in order to boost fixed investment), but that this comes at the expense of Chinese households whose savings deposits can actually lose value. Some have concluded that Chinese restrictive wage policies and controls on bank interest rates have dampened the level of household spending/consumption that would have been expected, given the rapid rate of China's economic growth.[106] **Figure A-8** shows Chinese personal disposable income as a percent of GDP for 2001 to 2010. The data indicate that this figure declined from 2001 to 2008, grew in 2009, but fell in 2010. Over the past ten years, personal disposable income as a percent of GDP fell from 47.5% to 40.8%. This indicates that Chinese households did not benefit as much from China's economic growth as other sectors of the economy. Many economists contend that the goal of rebalancing the Chinese economy toward greater reliance on personal consumption can not be achieved until the central government eliminates distortive economic policies that favor firms over households.

Figure A-8. Chinese Personal Disposal Income as a Percent of GDP: 2001-2010

(percent)

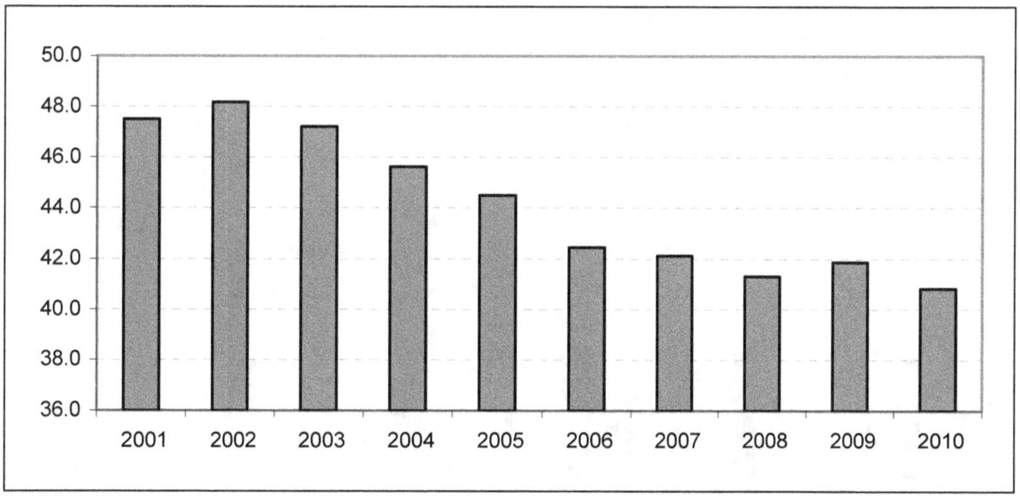

Source: EIU database.

Sources of China's Economic Growth

The sources of China's real GDP growth from 2005-2010 are shown in **Figure A-9**. Gross fixed investment (some of which is linked to tradable sectors) was the largest contributor to its real GDP growth over this period. The sharp growth in fixed investment in 2009 appears to reflect the results of the Chinese government's $586 billion stimulus package and its monetary easing policy that encouraged banks to expand lending—a significant amount of which is believed to have gone

---

[106] Chinese house consumption is also repressed because of the lack of an adequate social safety net. This forces them to maintain a high rate of savings in order to pay for medical costs, education, and future retirement costs (if they don't have a pension).

to infrastructure projects. In 2009, changes to net exports in China were a drag on the Chinese economy, while in 2010 they provided a modest contribution to GDP growth.

The next few years could be a critical period for China's economic policymakers. A number of economists have questioned the quality of China's massive investment efforts over the past two years and the ability of local government to repay the loans they took out to fund major investment projects. Thus, the importance of fixed investment to China's economic growth over the next few year could decline. The Chinese government's 12th Five Year Plan (2011-2015) states that rebalancing the economy, promoting consumer demand, boosting rural incomes, addressing income disparity (such as boosting wages), promoting the development of the services sector, and expanding social welfare programs (such as education, social security, and health care) will be major priorities. Such policies, if implemented, could provide a significant boost to consumer spending. Based on China's historical economic model, it will likely take several years for a significant rebalancing of the Chinese economy to occur. In addition, many economists have raised concerns that, as China's major trading partners, such as the United States and Europe, begin to experience more rapid economic growth, their demand for Chinese products will increase, which could discourage China's government from following through on economic reforms necessary to promote a rebalancing of the economy.

Figure A-9. Chinese Real GDP Growth and Sources of GDP Growth: 2005-2010

(percent and percentage points)

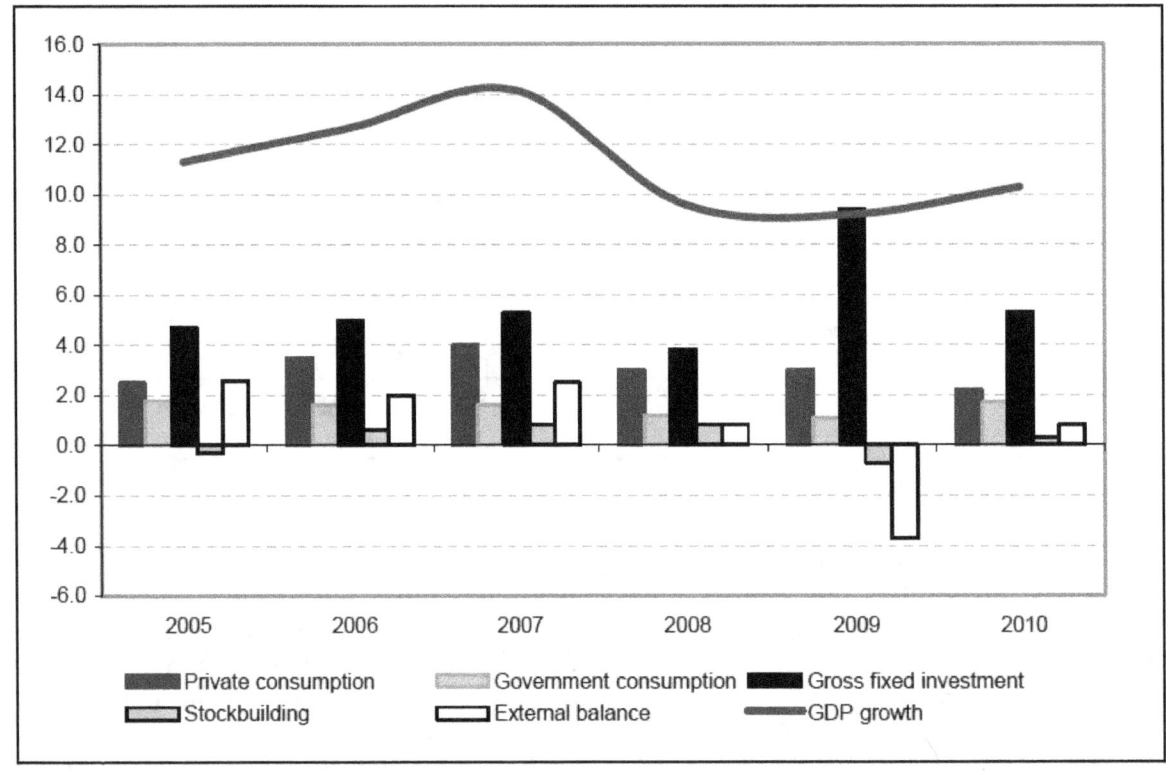

Source: Economist Intelligence Unit.

Author Contact Information

Wayne M. Morrison
Specialist in Asian Trade and Finance
wmorrison@crs.loc.gov, 7-7767

Marc Labonte
Specialist in Macroeconomic Policy
mlabonte@crs.loc.gov, 7-0640